Martin Luther and the German Reformation

Anthem Perspectives in History

Titles in the Anthem Perspectives in History series combine a thematic overview with analyses of key areas, topics or personalities in history. The series is targeted at high-achieving A Level, International Baccalaureate and Advanced Placement pupils, first-year undergraduates and an intellectually curious audience.

A History of Ireland, 1800–1922
Theatres of Disorder?
Hilary Larkin

Britain in India, 1858–1947
Lionel Knight

Disraeli and the Art of Victorian Politics
Second Edition
Ian St John

Disraeli and the Art of Victorian Politics
Ian St John

Gladstone and the Logic of Victorian Politics
Ian St John

King John
An Underrated King
Graham E. Seel

The Creation of Modern China, 1894–2008
The Rise of a World Power
Iain Robertson Scott

Martin Luther and the German Reformation

Rob Sorensen

ANTHEM PRESS

Anthem Press
An imprint of Wimbledon Publishing Company
www.anthempress.com

This edition first published in UK and USA 2016
by ANTHEM PRESS
75–76 Blackfriars Road, London SE1 8HA, UK
or PO Box 9779, London SW19 7ZG, UK
and
244 Madison Ave #116, New York, NY 10016, USA

© Rob Sorensen 2016

The moral right of the authors has been asserted.

All rights reserved. Without limiting the rights under copyright reserved above,
no part of this publication may be reproduced, stored or introduced into
a retrieval system, or transmitted, in any form or by any means
(electronic, mechanical, photocopying, recording or otherwise),
without the prior written permission of both the copyright
owner and the above publisher of this book.

British Library Cataloguing-in-Publication Data
A catalogue record for this book is available from the British Library.

Library of Congress Cataloging-in-Publication Data
Names: Sorensen, Robert A. (Robert Allen), 1951– author.
Title: Martin Luther and the German Reformation / Rob Sorensen.
Description: New York: Anthem Press, 2016. |
Includes bibliographical references and index.
Identifiers: LCCN 2016021079 | ISBN 9781783085651 (pbk.: alk. paper)
Subjects: LCSH: Luther, Martin, 1483–1546. | Reformation.
Classification: LCC BR332.5.S63 2016 | DDC 284.1092 [B]—dc23
LC record available at https://lccn.loc.gov/2016021079

ISBN-13: 9 781 7830 8565 1 (Pbk)
ISBN-10: 1 78308 565 7 (Pbk)

This title is also available as an e-book.

CONTENTS

Definition of Key Terms   ix

Introduction   1

1. Context   5
   1.1   The Late Medieval Church   6
   1.2   Crises of the Late Middle Ages   8
       1.2.1   Famine, plague and revolt   8
       1.2.2   Church schism   9
       1.2.3   Early reform movements   10
       1.2.4   The impact of humanism   11
   1.3   The Holy Roman Empire   12

2. Luther's Early Life   13
   2.1   Family and Early Childhood   13
       2.1.1   Young man Luther   14
   2.2   Early Education   15
   2.3   Nominalism   16
   2.4   Monk and Professor   17
   2.5   Justification by Faith   19

3. The Accidental Reformer   23
   3.1   The Indulgence Controversy   23
       3.1.1   What is an indulgence?   23
       3.1.2   Tetzel's plenary indulgence   24
       3.1.3   Did Luther actually post the *95 Theses*?   26
       3.1.4   Power politics   26
   3.2   The Heidelberg Disputation   30
   3.3   Friends in High Places   31

3.4		The Leipzig Debate	34
3.5		1520: The Decisive Year	36
	3.5.1	Excommunication	36
	3.5.2	Political support for Luther	37
	3.5.3	The key writings of 1520	38
3.6		The Diet of Worms	42

4. Conflict and Reform — 45
- 4.1 A Year of Exile — 45
  - 4.1.1 The Wartburg — 45
  - 4.1.2 The Bible in German — 47
  - 4.1.3 Radicalization of the reform movement — 48
  - 4.1.4 Return from exile — 50
- 4.2 The Peasants' War — 52
- 4.3 Zwingli and the Conflict over the Eucharist — 55
- 4.4 Erasmus and the Bondage of the Will — 57
- 4.5 The Augsburg Confession — 60

5. A New Way to Be a Christian — 65
- 5.1 Basic Themes in Luther's Theology — 65
  - 5.1.1 Justification by faith alone — 65
  - 5.1.2 The authority of scripture — 67
  - 5.1.3 The priesthood of all believers — 69
  - 5.1.4 The sacraments — 70
  - 5.1.5 Two kingdoms — 71
- 5.2 Marriage and Domestic Life — 72
- 5.3 The Development of the Lutheran Church — 75
- 5.4 Music — 77

6. The Final Years — 79
- 6.1 Home Life — 79
- 6.2 Physical and Emotional Illnesses — 81
- 6.3 Polemics and Controversies — 82
  - 6.3.1 Islam and the Turks — 83
  - 6.3.2 The question of the Jews — 84
  - 6.3.3 Philip of Hesse and bigamy — 86
- 6.4 The End — 87

7. The World Luther Made — 91
- 7.1 Long-Term Impacts — 91
  - 7.1.1 The spread of Lutheranism — 91
  - 7.1.2 The growth of individualism — 93
  - 7.1.3 Nationalism and politics — 94

	7.1.4	Social welfare and education	97
	7.1.5	Women and the family	99
7.2	Questions about Luther's Legacy		101
	7.2.1	Antinomianism—does human behavior matter at all?	102
	7.2.2	Why was Luther successful?	104
	7.2.3	How "Lutheran" was Luther?	105
7.3	Concluding Thoughts		107

For Further Study	109
Notes	111
Bibliography	117
Index	121

DEFINITION OF KEY TERMS

ANFECHTUNG: A word used by Luther to describe his spiritual struggles. It can mean "temptation," "trial" or "assault."

ANTINOMIANISM: The idea that righteous behavior is unnecessary because the grace of God can save you regardless of your sinfulness.

BAPTISM: One of the traditional Christian sacraments, baptism is a ceremony in which a person is immersed in or sprinkled with water to signify the forgiveness of sins and admission into the church. In the sixteenth century, baptism was almost universally a ceremony performed on newborn infants.

CARDINAL: A high official in the Catholic hierarchy, appointed by the pope as one of his chief assistants and advisors. Cardinals also elect a new pope upon the death of the previous pope.

CATECHISM: A short instructional work designed to teach people the basics of Christianity.

CLERICAL CELIBACY: The idea that members of the clergy ought to remain unmarried and should refrain from sexual relations.

CONCILIARISM: A late fifteenth-century movement that claimed that supreme religious authority lay with church councils rather than in the person of the pope.

ELECTOR: One of seven princes of the Holy Roman Empire who could vote in elections for emperor.

EUCHARIST: One of the traditional seven sacraments. The Eucharist is the symbolic meal of bread and wine that were also mystically Christ's body and blood.

EXCOMMUNICATION: The official act of revoking a person's membership in the church.

FORENSIC JUSTIFICATION: The idea that a believer is declared righteous, but not actually made righteous.

GOSPEL: Literally "good news," the term was used by Luther to refer to the central teachings of Christianity and particularly the doctrine of justification by faith alone.

HERESY: Belief or teaching that is contradictory to the official teachings of the church.

HUMANISM: A movement seeking to revive the culture and scholarship of ancient Greece and Rome through returning to the original sources and languages. Humanists also emphasized the value and ability of the individual human being.

ICONOCLASM: The opposition to the use of images in Christian worship.

INDULGENCE: Official remittance of penance for sins, available for purchase from the church.

JUSTIFICATION BY FAITH: Luther's central doctrine—that sinners can be reconciled with God not through any act on their part, but rather by having faith that God will act to reconcile them with Himself.

MASS: Can refer either to the Eucharist, or to the church service in which the central element is the celebration of the Eucharist.

MONASTICISM: A religious commitment to poverty, chastity and obedience.

ORTHODOX CHURCH: A Christian church, prominent in Eastern Europe and the Middle East. The Orthodox are a historic church not connected with the Roman Catholic Church.

POPE: The title for the Bishop of Rome, the official leader of the Catholic Church.

PENANCE: An act, assigned by a priest, to atone for sin.

PURGATORY: A place for the Christian dead to complete their acts of penance before being allowed to enter heaven.

REAL PRESENCE: The idea that Christ's actual body and blood are present in the Eucharist. Unlike transubstantiation, belief in the real presence does not necessarily imply that the bread and wine are completely replaced.

SACRAMENT: One of the seven rituals believed to convey God's grace to believers.

THEOSIS: The teaching, associated with Eastern Orthodox Christianity, that the believer becomes, through faith, united with God.

TRANSUBSTANTIATION: The doctrine that held that the bread and wine of the Eucharist actually become, in their entirety, Jesus's real body and blood.

VERNACULAR: The common language spoken by the people.

VESTMENT: A ceremonial garment worn by a priest during church services.

INTRODUCTION

Sunt bona, sunt quaedam mediocria, sunt mala plura
Quae legis hic: aliter non fit, Avite, liber.
—Martial, Epigram 1.16

Martin Luther is unquestionably one of the most prominent figures of the past millennium, and there is certainly no shortage of books about him. Yet he remains a fascinating and enigmatic figure. He is in many ways foreign to twenty-first century sensibilities, but he continues to speak deeply to many people—myself included—nearly five hundred years after his death. He introduced Europeans to a God who was not concerned with their good works, their personal piety, or their religious observation, but who simply reconciled sinners to himself by grace. In doing so, Luther initiated a theological revolution that splintered the Christian church and ushered in the modern world. This is his story.

Issues and Problems in Luther Study

A new treatment of Luther is an enormous task—far larger than I had anticipated when I first began to write this book. Nevertheless, I soldiered on to produce the volume that you now hold in your hands. A part of the problem is the immense volume of source material there is to work with. Luther's own writings fill more than a hundred large volumes in the standard Weimar edition used by scholars. Only some of these have been translated into English, but the standard English translation still fills 55 large volumes. In addition to this, there are tens of thousands of books and articles about Luther's life and thought, with hundreds more coming out each year. Even the most dedicated scholar can only hope to absorb a small fraction of this material.

An additional challenge is the fact that, unlike many theologians, Luther never developed his thought in writing in anything like a systematic fashion. Most of his writings are direct responses to particular events in his life, making it difficult to understand his theological and philosophical views without first having a concrete understanding of his life and times. Thus, any student of Luther's thought must first master the intricacies of Luther's life, and have at least a passing acquaintance with the political and social history of the early sixteenth century.

And there are also interpretive problems with the sources themselves. Contemporary accounts of Luther's life are written either by Luther's friends or by his enemies. In both cases, their reliability is open to question. All of Luther's autobiographical writings are retrospective—written many years after the events that they record and likely colored by the intervening events of his life. The most interesting source of information about the mature Luther is his *Table Talk*—notes taken by admirers as Luther lectured, conversed and joked while dining with his students. Although these notes give us a rounded picture of Luther as a man, there are legitimate questions about their accuracy, and in any event, the nature of their composition render them at best a selective account of Luther's life.

Luther's way of looking at the world is also quite different from that which is typical in the twenty-first century. Luther sees everything in his world through theological lenses. Those of us who live in a secular era often find this difficult to grab hold of. Luther knew the Bible deeply and expected that his readers would share his familiarity. He would be shocked by the modern tendency to separate the world into secular and sacred spheres, and would object mightily to the religious pluralism that reigns in most Western democracies today. Luther took his faith very seriously—to the extent that he seems almost crazy to people raised to assume that secularism is the most normal way to view the world.

The great Luther scholar Bernhard Lohse once suggested that every biographer of Luther must take a personal position on Luther and recognize that his or her own particular value judgments will affect the final product.[1] This judgment, while true of all historical scholarship, is particularly true for those writing about Luther. I am, of course, no exception. I write as a Lutheran, and as one who admires Luther in many ways. Nevertheless, I recognize that Luther is not a cardboard saint, and I am troubled by some of his polemics. As such, although I have tried to maintain an appropriate level of critical distance, the reader can judge whether my own admiration for Luther has colored my judgment.

About This Book

This book is not intended to be an exhaustive treatment of Luther or of the Protestant Reformation. It is, instead, intended to introduce the reader to the basics of Luther's life and thought, and to provide direction for further study. Although written primarily for high-school and college students, I hope that the general public will also find it useful. Throughout the book, I make reference to English sources that should be readily available to anyone with access to a good library. Those who are interested in a deeper treatment, or who wish to pursue more advanced study of Luther, should consult the bibliographic essay at the end of this book.

Chapter 1

CONTEXT

Today, some 500 years after he lived, Martin Luther is regularly considered by historians to be one of the most important figures of the last millennium. *Life* magazine, for instance, in its survey of the most important people and events of the last thousand years, listed Luther third, behind only Thomas Edison and Christopher Columbus. The Protestant Reformation, sparked by Luther's actions, was ranked by *Life* as the third-most-important event of the millennium.[1] He is regularly studied by high school students in their history classes. He is the subject of countless books, and even of popular movies. Few would contest the fact that he is one of the most significant figures in European history.

However, few people in the late fifteenth century—the time of Luther's birth—would have expected young Martin to achieve anything near this kind of greatness. Luther himself, near the end of his career, looked back on his life and explained how his fame had taken him by surprise:

> I am the son of a peasant. My great-grandfather, grandfather, and father were peasants... I should have become a superintendent, a bailiff or the like in the village, a servant with authority over a few... that I [earned a good education], that I became a monk which brought shame upon me as it bitterly annoyed my father—that I and the Pope came to blows, that I married an apostate nun; who would have read this in the stars? Who would have prophesied it?[2]

The baby boy born to Hans and Margaret Luther on a rainy November evening in 1483 certainly did not seem like a potential world leader. He was from a peasant family of modest income. He had no influential connections in imperial or local politics. He lived in the small town of Eisleben, in a relatively unimportant corner of eastern Germany. Nevertheless, Luther would come to be one of the most important religious thinkers of all time, and his actions and ideas would deeply influence the future of Europe and the world. This is the story of how this apparently insignificant baby became a world-changing figure. In order to understand Luther's journey, however, we must begin a bit before his birth and examine the world into which he was born.

1.1 The Late Medieval Church

The world into which Luther was born was a deeply religious one. Those of us who live in a largely secular age may find it hard to comprehend how thoroughly the Christian church influenced and governed the lives of medieval Europeans. For them, the church calendar organized their life experiences. Sundays, set aside for worship and rest, broke up the daily grind of work and church festivals, and saints' days provided an annual rhythm of work and play. The major events of a person's life were marked by the church ceremonies of baptism, marriage, and last rites. The church was the center of learning and education—often the local parish priest was the only person in a village who could read and write. People got their only news of the wider world from the pulpit, where royal decrees and other news were read. Physically the great cathedrals and other churches dominated the skylines of medieval cities. No area of life was outside the influence of the church.

The church was a truly international body; in many ways, churches were independent of secular governments. The head of the church was the pope, who generally resided in Rome, and who claimed to be the direct successor to the apostle Peter, to whom Jesus had entrusted the "keys to the kingdom."[3] The popes often claimed spectacular authority, but they were not always able to actually exercise the power that they claimed. Medieval history featured regular conflicts between the papacy and various kings and emperors regarding who possessed the higher power. The pope was the final arbiter of doctrine, and the ultimate authority in church governance.

In the late fifteenth century, the popes were particularly jealous of their authority. Part of the reason for this was the lingering influence of conciliarism, a movement that sought to limit the power of the pope. The conciliarists suggested that the ultimate authority in the church was not the pope, but rather a council made up of leading bishops and representing the church as a whole. This model developed a vision of the church as a kind of constitutional monarchy, in which the power of the pope was tempered by his responsibility to a church council. The popes had been battling the conciliarists for many years, but the conciliarists were losing ground fast during the later fifteenth century, and their movement was formally condemned at the Fifth Lateran Council, which ran from 1512 to 1517. It is significant that Luther—who also questioned whether the pope ought to have ultimate authority—was beginning to be prominent at just the same time as the conciliar movement was formally condemned. It may help to explain why Luther's opponents were so dogmatically committed to papal authority.

The popes ruled over a large and complex hierarchy of clergy. Directly below the pope were a group of officials called cardinals. These were appointed by the pope and were often styled "princes of the church." The cardinals served as papal ambassadors and assistants, and were the pope's closest advisors. When a pope died, the cardinals chose the new pope, usually out of their own number. Next in line in the church hierarchy were the archbishops and bishops who oversaw the church in specific geographical areas called dioceses. These bishops were charged with overseeing the clergy and property of the diocese, as well as administering certain important sacraments. Very often, bishops were wealthy men from important families who played significant roles in power politics. At the very bottom of the hierarchy were the parish priests, who performed the offices of the local pastor. The duties of the local priests included saying masses, administering most of the sacraments, comforting the sick and dying, hearing confessions, and generally functioning as spiritual caretaker for their congregations.

Alongside this administrative hierarchy was a second group of clergy—the monks and nuns. These were men and women who lived apart from the world, having taken vows of poverty, chastity, and obedience. Monks and nuns devoted themselves to worship, labor, and study in the hopes of gaining a closer relationship with God. It was from this part of the church that Luther was to draw his ideas, and from which he would challenge the pope himself.

The chief problem that this elaborate hierarchy was designed to solve was how the sinful individual could be made right with God. The key to this reconciliation, for the medieval church, was the system of sacraments. The church taught that in order to be saved, individuals needed grace, which was delivered through the sacraments. Because the sacraments were administered by the church, the sacramental system served to increase the power of the church hierarchy—because only the institutional church held the power to reconcile sinners with God. The most significant of the sacraments were Baptism, the Eucharist, and Penance.

Baptism was a ceremonial washing that was usually administered to infants. Since an unbaptized child could not enter heaven, in an age of high infant mortality, most parents had their babies baptized immediately after their birth. Baptism cleansed the soul from original sin and initiated the baptized into the church. Following Baptism, the most important sacrament was the

Eucharist. This was a ceremonial meal of bread and wine, which were also mystically Christ's body and blood. The Eucharist was the central element of the mass, and would be performed during every church service. Most Europeans, however, did not personally participate in the Eucharist except on very special occasions. The third important sacrament was the practice of penance. This involved confessing one's sins to a priest. Upon hearing the confession, the priest would assign an act of penance, by means of which the sinner could atone for his sins.

Throughout the middle ages, there were numerous (and often ponderously complicated) disagreements among theologians about the precise nature and function of the sacraments. We need not explore these conflicts, however. To understand Luther, we need only observe that medieval Christians generally believed two very significant things about the sacraments. First, the sacraments were seen as absolutely necessary for salvation. Without the grace that was mediated to the sinner through the sacraments, there would be no hope of ascending to heaven. Second, medieval Christians believed that the sacraments were more than just symbols. Christ was truly, physically, tangibly present in the sacrament. The last was particularly true for the Eucharist, which did not merely *represent* Christ's body and blood, but actually *became* Christ's real body and real blood.

1.2 Crises of the Late Middle Ages

The powerful influence of the church was shaken (but not, ultimately, broken) in the fourteenth and fifteenth centuries by a series of substantial crises. These crises caused many people to question their assumptions. The church was unable to resolve—or in some cases to even adequately explain—these crises. This contributed to a widespread demand for reform of the church. By 1483, when Luther was born, Europeans had a definite tendency to be disillusioned with the church.

1.2.1 *Famine, plague and revolt*

The fourteenth century opened with a series of poor harvests, which led to a severe food shortage throughout Europe. Without enough food to provide for a growing population, many died of starvation and malnutrition. The famine also weakened those who survived, making the population particularly susceptible to the devastating plague that swept through Europe between 1347 and 1351.

The Black Death, as this plague came to be known, killed more than a third of the population of Europe. Doctors were not able to cure the disease or slow its spread. The church could not explain the presence of a catastrophe of such an unprecedented scale, and many people saw the plague as God's judgment upon a sinful world. The plague would continue to break out periodically in various parts of Europe for the next two centuries.

As the plague was sweeping through Europe, peasant revolts were causing additional devastation. Because so many were killed by the plague, there was a shortage of agricultural workers. This meant that the surviving peasants saw their labor become more highly valued than it had been in the past, and they could hold out for higher wages. Many landowners found it increasingly difficult to find enough workers to bring in the harvest. This led to harsh measures on the part of the lords, who tried to force the remaining peasants to do more work. The peasants resented this treatment, which often violated traditional arrangements. Many took up arms in revolt. The authorities often crushed these revolts mercilessly, contributing to a simmering tension between peasants and their lords. This dynamic made its way into Luther's life in 1525, when he was involved in one of the most devastating of these peasant revolts—and one that Luther's teachings may have helped to spark.

1.2.2 Church schism

The loss of confidence that grew out of the devastation of the plague and revolt was exacerbated by a serious internal conflict within the church itself. The pope held the important office of Bishop of Rome, and was generally expected to reside in that city. But in 1309, the newly elected pope, Clement V, moved from Rome to Avignon, a city in southern France. Clement was widely seen as subservient to the French king, a fact which frustrated Christians who thought that the church ought to be above the fray of national politics. The next seven popes would rule from Avignon, where the papacy gained a reputation for worldliness and corruption. The respect in which the papacy had been held during the earlier middle ages declined steadily during the Avignon papacy. Many theologians called upon the popes to return to Rome and to abandon their worldly ways.

Pope Gregory VII ultimately moved the papacy back to Rome in 1377, but died within months. As the cardinals met to decide upon a new pope, crowds surrounded the papal palace demanding the election of an Italian as pope. The cardinals consented, and the new pope, Urban VI, was an Italian. But the cardinals, most of whom were accustomed to the relatively luxurious atmosphere of Avignon, clashed with Urban, an ascetic who tried to limit the power of money and bribery in the papal curia. Several months after Urban's election, a group of cardinals returned to Avignon, declared that the election of Urban was invalid because the cardinals had been under duress when they made their decision, and elected another pope, who took the name Clement VII.

This meant that there were now two rival popes: Clement in Avignon and Urban in Rome. For the next forty years, there would be two popes, competing with one another for the allegiances of kings and rulers. The rival popes excommunicated one another and each declared that they alone were the true pope. Before the schism was ended by the Council of Constance in 1415, much of Europe had lost respect for the papacy as an institution. The conciliar movement's skepticism of papal power has some roots in the dissatisfaction with the papacy that emerged out of the Avignon papacy and the papal schism.

1.2.3 Early reform movements

The crises of the fourteenth and fifteenth centuries were seen by many as an indication of God's judgment on a sinful society. The only way to remove this judgment was to thoroughly reform the church and society. Many saw the worldliness of the papacy as a further indication that reform was necessary. Reform of the church was a common theme in late medieval writings, and several important thinkers openly called for dramatic reforms.

The most significant of these early advocates of reform was John Wyclif, a professor at Oxford. Wyclif argued that the final authority in matters of doctrine and practice was not the pope, but the Bible. Because of this, he advocated translating the Bible—traditionally only available in the standard Latin version—into the vernacular languages so that individual Christians could read it. He also argued that the authority of any clergy was based on their moral example. Thus church leaders—including popes—who behaved in a worldly manner could not legitimately exercise any spiritual power. The church, he said, should not pursue worldly wealth, nor should clergy be involved in politics. All of these proposals bear striking similarities to the conclusions Luther would reach during the 1520s.

Wyclif's ideas spread to Bohemia, where they were picked up by a preacher and academic named Jan Hus. Wyclif, who worked in England some distance away from the centers of power, attracted little attention from the papacy during his lifetime. He was also protected to some degree by the English nobility, who saw his criticism of the church as a potential opportunity to increase their own power. Hus, on the other hand, lived in Prague, near the center of Europe, and had more limited support from his own government. When Hus began to preach ideas similar to Wyclif's in Prague, church authorities took instant notice. Hus was called before the Council of Constance in 1415, and when he refused to recant he was burned at the stake as a heretic. Like Hus,

Luther would be asked by the church to recant—and you can be sure that the fate of Hus was on Luther's mind when he was defending his ideas before his ecclesiastical superiors.

1.2.4 The impact of humanism

Another element contributing to the instability of the late middle ages was the growth and spread of humanism. Humanism was a movement that sought to revive the culture and scholarship of ancient Greece and Rome. Humanists generally advocated a return to the original sources—rather than read medieval Latin translations of the Greek classics, the humanists learned Greek and read the original. This focus on the original sources led Christian humanists to focus their attention on the text of the Bible, rather than the commentaries and canon law that had developed during the middle ages. By contrasting their own age with what they saw as the ideal world of classical antiquity, humanists also gained a powerful tool with which to critique the shortcomings of the late medieval church and government.

Another element of the humanist movement was an increased emphasis on the value and ability of the individual human being. This was the dynamic that led, in Italy, to the great flourishing of art and literature during the Renaissance. It was also a powerful idea. The idea that it was the individual—rather than the family, the guild, or some other social group—that was central bears a striking similarity to the idea of the priesthood of all believers that Luther would later adopt as a central part of his theological program.

Humanism began in Italy, but it rapidly spread northward. By the time of Luther, humanism was flourishing in Germany. Humanists such as the famed Dutch scholar Desiderius Erasmus saw the revival of the classics as a potent tool for reforming the Christian church—which they tended to see as largely corrupt. By adopting a program of reform that involved a return to the Biblical sources and a thorough training in the liberal arts, Erasmus hoped to restore the church to its original splendor. Like the religious reform movement that Luther would initiate, Erasmus and other humanists sought to enact moral reforms, to limit the arbitrary power of the papacy, and to return European society to its traditional—but now lost—foundations.

Taken together, the impact of plague, famine, church schism, and humanism created an atmosphere in which Europe was ripe for a thorough reformation. Luther was born into this complex, crisis-laden world. Thus, when Luther began his program of reform, he was building on established foundations with the church and providing a way for people to explain and resolve some of the crises that had racked Europe for two centuries.

1.3 The Holy Roman Empire

Luther was also born into a particular place. In the late fifteenth century, the territory that we now know as Germany and Austria was governed by an unusual political entity known as the Holy Roman Empire. In 1495, the Empire was made up of more than 350 independent states, all of which were theoretically subordinate to the Holy Roman Emperor. In practice, however, the emperor's actual control over the rulers of these smaller territories was minimal. Unlike the hereditary kings of England or France, the Holy Roman Emperors were elected by a panel of seven princes, each of whom held the title "elector." Because of this, the emperors were forced to grant the princes a great deal of independent authority. Any attempt to subdue the princes might cost the emperor the chance to have his sons or relatives succeed him.

The division of power between the emperor and the princes made governing the Empire difficult. Imperial edicts that went against the interests of the princes could prove difficult to enforce. Furthermore, independent imperial cities like Nuremberg and Augsburg were trying to carve out a third way that was independent of both emperor and hereditary princes.

Because of the decentralized nature of the German government, the church played an unusually significant role in the government of the Empire—far more so than in most other European states. Three of the German electors were bishops, giving the church a very strong voice in imperial politics. The weak central government allowed the church to tax Germans more heavily than it could manage in other states whose centralized monarchies were better able to resist the papacy. This strong presence of the church in German politics gave many of the secular German princes a strong incentive to support church reform movements, because by opposing the power of the church hierarchy, they hoped to protect their own political autonomy against the central government.

So when Luther was born, Europe was ready for a reformer. Dissatisfaction with the church was growing, and crises were challenging people's assumptions about God and the world. Unrest was particularly strong in Germany, and Germany had a government that was least likely to provide strong resistance to reformers. So, young Martin was, in many ways, born in the right place at the right time.

Chapter 2

LUTHER'S EARLY LIFE

2.1 Family and Early Childhood

The crises and unrest of the late fifteenth century would have been far from the minds of Hans and Margaret Luther on the evening in 1483 when their son was born. The church, although under criticism, still dominated the lives of peasants like the Luthers. The first task of Hans Luther upon the birth of his son would have been arranging for the baby's baptism. So, as soon as it was practical, Hans brought the boy to the local parish priest and presented him for baptism. Because the day of the baby's baptism—November 11—was the feast day of St. Martin of Tours, the baby was named Martin.

Hans and Margaret were peasants, and the young Martin grew up among the peasantry—a fact about which he later boasted. The Luthers were not destitute, however. Hans' father (and Martin's grandfather), Heine Luther, had been a moderately prosperous independent farmer in the village of Möhra. According to local custom, the youngest son inherited the entire family property. Since Hans was an older son, he wasn't able to inherit the family farm. Instead, he sought his fortunes in the copper mines of the nearby county of Mansfield. He first tried the mines in Eisleben, the largest city in the area. It was here that Martin was born. Hans was unable to advance in Eisleben, however, and about a year after Martin's birth, Hans moved his growing family to the smaller town of Mansfield, ten miles away. At Mansfield, Hans began to prosper in the mining industry. By 1491, he had become a partner in a mining company that ultimately would operate at least six copper mines and two copper smelters, a position that gave him a reasonable income and good opportunities for advancement. Young Martin may have experienced some moderate scarcity in his early youth, as Hans was beginning to make his way in the mining industry, but it seems unlikely that he would have ever known true poverty—at least personally.

Hans' wife, the former Margaret Lindemann, was a young woman from an established middle-class merchant family in Eisenach. Margaret's relatives included doctors, lawyers, university professors, and civil servants. Margaret's relatives were probably instrumental in helping Hans Luther secure the credit he would have needed to purchase his ownership stake in the copper mines. Martin's Lindemann relatives would be deeply influential in the young man's life. It seems likely that the Lindemanns encouraged the Luthers to send young Martin to school, and may have provided some of the money necessary to make that happen. So while Luther's claim to be born a peasant is true in the technical sense, we should not be misled into thinking that Luther grew up in poverty.

2.1.1 *Young man Luther*

There is little concrete evidence about Luther's early childhood, but some scholars have suggested that a key feature of his early life may have been a difficult relationship with his parents. Later in life, he recalled receiving several beatings as a child, which may have deeply affected the sensitive youth. He even suggests that the trauma of these punishments may have contributed to his later decision to become a monk:

> My parents kept me under very strict discipline, even to the point of making me timid. For the sake of a mere nut my mother beat me until the blood flowed. By such strict discipline they finally forced me into the monastery; though they meant it heartily well, I was only made timid by it.[1]

When he had children of his own, he remembered the strictness of his own upbringing and vowed to treat his own children differently.

This apparent tension between Luther and his parents led the Freudian psychologist Erik Erikson to write a noteworthy and controversial study of Luther's relationship with his father. In *Young Man Luther*, Erikson claimed that Luther's later criticism of the church had its roots in his own dysfunctional relationship with his father.[2] Basing his analysis on Luther's late-life recollections of parental punishments, Erikson concluded that Luther had been terrorized by his father as a child and grew up resentful and untrusting of his parents. Luther later transferred these feelings of hatred for his father to all other father figures, including God and the pope. Thus, he came to see God as a stern and hateful judge.

Even if Luther had a somewhat tempestuous relationship with his father, many recent scholars are skeptical of Erikson's conclusions. They point out that his psychological claims about Luther are based on very limited evidence and that Erikson ignores other relevant evidence that seems to indicate that the causes of Luther's problems with God and the church are more likely to be rooted in his religious beliefs than in any hatred for his parents.[3] Furthermore, physical discipline of the sort described by Luther was not uncommon in the late fifteenth century, and there is little evidence that Luther's relationship with his parents was extraordinary for its time. Young Martin seems to have been aware that his parents loved him and meant well by him, even while he regretted his father's sternness. As an adult, Luther's letters to his parents are filled with love and affection, and there is no indication of lingering bitterness.[4]

2.2 Early Education

Formal education was an uncommon privilege for the son of a peasant, even a relatively prosperous one like Hans Luther. Nevertheless, formal schooling would provide Martin with the opportunity to rise above the ranks of the peasantry and to earn a secure living as a lawyer or a government bureaucrat—all careers that Luther's Lindemann relatives had successfully achieved. So Luther entered the grammar school in Mansfield, where he learned Latin, the universal language of government and scholarship. He later complained that he had learned little from his early schooling, and was critical of the regular physical punishment meted out by his instructors. He did, however, learn enough Latin to advance to the next level of schooling. In 1496 or 1497, Luther left home to attend a boarding school in Magdeburg and after a short stay there moved to Eisenach, where his mother's family still lived, to complete his basic education. At Eisenach, Luther found sympathetic teachers and lifelong friends. He developed into an exceptional student. By the end of his career at Eisenach, Luther had a fluent command of Latin, a familiarity with the pagan and Christian classics, and a deep love for music and poetry.

In 1501, Luther enrolled in the University of Erfurt, where he completed his bachelor's degree in a single year, the minimum time allowed by the university. He immediately began to study for the Master of Arts degree, which he received in January 1505, ranking second in his class of seventeen. This degree entitled Luther to teach in the university's faculty of arts, and also was a prerequisite for admission to study for a degree in law, which was Luther's goal. Earning a master's degree was a considerable achievement, and one of which both Luther and his father were immensely proud. Hans even celebrated Martin's graduation with a gift of the entire *Corpus Juris Civilis*—the principal textbook for legal studies, and a very costly gift. Luther entered the law school at Erfurt in 1505, with the expectation of a profitable legal career, with which he could rise above his peasant origins and support his parents in their old age.

2.3 Nominalism

The faculty at Erfurt tended to hold a philosophical position called nominalism or the *via moderna*, which seems to have deeply influenced the young Luther. In particular, Luther absorbed the key idea that all theological and philosophical ideas should be tested by reason and experience, rather than by relying on traditional authorities. This concept—that scholars should base their study on their own reason and experience—encouraged nominalist theologians to question traditional medieval theology, and even to stand up to the power of the church hierarchy. Erfurt was an established center of nominalism well before Luther enrolled there in 1501. In fact, Johannes von Wesel, a member of Erfurt's theological faculty in the late fifteenth century, was imprisoned by the inquisition in 1479 for his willingness to challenge the church's teaching on indulgences—an issue that would later become key in Luther's own journey. Later in his life, Luther openly claimed to be an admirer of nominalist theologians such as William of Occam and Gabriel Biel and he proved willing to subject any claims—even those of his teachers—to the scrutiny of reason. "I demand arguments, not authorities," he wrote. "That is why I contradict even my own school of Occamists, which I have absorbed completely."[5]

A second significant element of the nominalist theology that Luther encountered at Erfurt was the argument that human beings could, through their moral actions, contribute to their own salvation. The argument is complicated, but can be summarized as follows. If sinners do the best they can to live moral, upright lives, God honors that effort by granting them the gift of grace that allows them to be saved. God does this not because the sinners have achieved moral perfection (which would be impossible), but because he honors their true efforts to do what is right. Thus, in a way, human beings cooperate with God in bringing about their own salvation. The doctrine also implies that human beings have the responsibility to do their best to live appropriately moral lives.[6]

Although Luther was a successful student, he was troubled by periodic attacks of conscience that he called *anfechtung*. The word is hard to render fully into English; it can mean "temptation," "trial," or even "assault." Some, following Erikson, have linked these attacks with Luther's poor relationship with his father, but this is at best a partial explanation. Luther later gave a vivid description of the experience:

> They were so great and so much like hell that no tongue could adequately express them, no pen could describe them, and one who had not himself experienced them could not believe them. And so great were they that,

if they had been sustained or had lasted for half an hour, even for one tenth of an hour he would have perished completely and all of his bones would have been reduced to ashes. At such a time, God seems terribly angry and with him the whole creation.[7]

Many scholars have tried to diagnose the source of these attacks in a medical condition, and it is true that Luther suffered from a number of ailments, including gallstones and angina. Erikson and others see the attacks as evidence of psychological trauma. But it is remarkably difficult to achieve a conclusive medical diagnosis for a man who died nearly 500 years ago. Luther himself never considers his *anfechtung* to be related to his medical conditions, which he speaks of quite frequently in his letters. Instead, he attributes a spiritual cause. The deepest cause of these attacks was, for Luther, the fact that he could not be confident of his own standing with God. Luther feared God's judgment and worried that he would not be saved. To a large extent, Luther's bouts of *anfechtung* demonstrate how deeply he had absorbed the nominalism of Erfurt. He was skeptical of simply accepting the claims of church authorities that he would be saved through the mechanisms that the church had put into place—he insisted, instead, on reason and experience for the assurance of God's grace. But he found that his experience was not of God's grace, but rather of God's judgment. Furthermore, according to nominalist theology, God's gift of grace to sinners was dependent upon the sinner doing his best to uphold God's moral laws. But when Luther looked into his heart, he was not satisfied that he had, in fact, done everything that was in his power. Even more troubling for Luther was the thought that, when he reflected on his deepest motivations, he feared that his moral efforts were not motivated by love for God, but instead by a fear of God's punishment. He feared that he would never be able to please God.

2.4 Monk and Professor

To his friends and family, it would have seemed that Luther had his life in good order during the summer of 1505. He was a successful student, and seemed to have an excellent career in law or the university ahead of him. But his heart was uneasy. He feared God's judgment, and doubted that his efforts to please God would ever find success. In July 1505, shortly after starting his legal studies, he returned to Mansfeld for a short visit with his parents. While walking back to Erfurt he was overtaken by a severe thunderstorm, and a sudden bolt of lightning struck the ground next to him, knocking him over. In this moment, the fear of God and his own sense of unworthiness overcame him. He prayed, but not to God. Instead, he turned to St. Anne, the patron saint of miners, and probably a figure of some devotion within the Luther household. He bargained for his life—if St. Anne would save him from the storm, he promised to leave school and become a monk.[8] It was a rash promise, and one that he almost immediately regretted. His friends tried to get him to change his mind, and his father was furious.[9] Nevertheless, Luther kept his promise. He bid his friends farewell, gave away his possessions, and entered the life of a monk.

There is something odd about a young man with a promising future giving up everything to enter the monastery. It seems probable that Luther became a monk primarily because he hoped that living an austere religious life would help him to overcome his uncertainty about his salvation—rather than to simply fulfill a somewhat rash promise made under duress. Luther clearly hoped that monasticism would help to resolve the bouts of despair he had been suffering. Later in life, he recalled during a sermon that "I thought: 'Oh, if I enter a cloister and serve God in cowl and tonsure, He will reward and welcome me.'"[10]

There were several different monasteries in Erfurt. Luther chose the Augustinians, who had a reputation for scholarship and sincerity. It was also one of the strictest of the monastic orders. He was probably most familiar with the Augustinians as well, since many of the brothers at the Augustinian cloister were also members of the university faculty, and because the order's philosophical and theological positions were similar to those he had learned at the university.

Luther was an observant monk, and went above and beyond the requirements of his order. "I almost fasted myself to death," he recalled, "for again and again I went for three days without taking a drop of water or a morsel of food. I was very serious about it."[11] He was constantly anxious about the state of his soul. He would spend hours confessing his sins to his superiors, trying zealously to remember and confess every sinful thought and deed. His confessor and close friend Johan von Staupitz, after one lengthy confession in which Luther had confessed nothing truly consequential, joked that Luther ought to try committing a real sin before his next confession.[12] Despite his best efforts, though, he still did not find the peace that he was looking for. "Though I lived as a monk without reproach," he recalled, "I felt that I was a sinner before God with an extremely disturbed conscience."[13]

This disturbed conscience is seen particularly clearly in his recollection of the first time he performed the mass. A little more than a year after Luther entered the monastery, he was formally ordained to the priesthood, giving him the authority to perform the sacrament of the Eucharist. As the central action of the mass, the presiding priest would raise the bread and wine and speak the words of institution: "This is my body" and "This is my blood."

At this point, the bread and wine would be mysteriously transformed into the true, actual flesh and blood of Christ and could, as such, mediate God's grace to penitent sinners. When the newly ordained Father Martin said his first mass, he was so nervous that he could hardly continue. He was struck with the terror of standing in the presence of God, of handling Christ's actual body—all while he felt himself to be utterly sinful and far from God.[14]

The first mass was also probably the first time that Luther had seen his father since his entry into the monastery. Hans had come to see his son's first mass, bringing 20 men with him, as well as a substantial donation to the cloister of 20 gold gulden. His father's presence likely added to Luther's nervousness. When the two spoke after the mass, it was clear that the relationship between them was tense. Martin asked his father whether his new role as a priest was not in fact better than the career in the law that his father had envisioned for him. Hans acidly replied by asking whether Luther remembered that the fifth commandment was to honor one's father and mother.[15]

Despite all of this, Luther rose quickly through the ranks of the Augustinian order. He was routinely given additional responsibilities and promoted to positions of influence. In 1510 he was one of two monks chosen to represent the Erfurt Augustinians at a meeting in Rome. The business that brought him to Rome only occupied a small portion of his time, so he was free to take in the sights and sounds of the city. He was shocked by the rampant immorality that he observed and was deeply troubled by the worldliness and greed of the church officials that he encountered.[16]

In late 1511, Staupitz assigned Luther to a position as professor of theology at the newly founded university at Wittenberg. Luther objected, feeling himself incapable of such a calling. Nevertheless, Staupitz insisted, and Luther began preparations for his doctorate. Before long he packed up to move to Wittenberg. Although it was the capital of the Elector of Saxony, Wittenberg was not a major city. Its university was something of an academic backwater in 1512. It had only been founded in 1502, and since then had had trouble recruiting quality faculty. In October 1512, Luther was formally granted the degree of Doctor of Theology and thereupon began to lecture at Wittenberg on various books of the Bible, beginning with the Psalms.

2.5 Justification by Faith

Although Luther was not happy to be sent to Wittenberg, Staupitz' decision to encourage the uneasy young monk to take up an academic career turned out to be the best thing for resolving Luther's questions. Any teacher can attest that the pressure of teaching a subject often requires the teacher to reflect more deeply on the subject matter to be taught. Thus, when he was assigned to teach the Bible, he began to read the Bible more deeply and more thoughtfully than he had before. As he lectured, first on the Psalms and later on St. Paul's epistles to the Galatians and the Romans, he studied these books assiduously. As he became more deeply familiar with the Biblical texts, his view of how human beings relate to God began to shift. He began to feel that the theology he had been taught was insufficient. Rather than seeing salvation as a sort of contract between God and humans in which God granted graced to those who fulfilled their side of the contract by doing their best to fulfill his commandments, Luther gradually began to see salvation as a promise from God—no strings attached.

As a professor, one of Luther's main concerns was the problem of God's righteousness. He knew that God was righteous. He also knew that he himself was not righteous. At Erfurt, he had absorbed the nominalist idea that the sinner had to do his best to live righteously in order to merit God's grace, but when he looked at his own motives and efforts, he could never be satisfied that he had done his very best. There was always more that he could have done. Furthermore, and perhaps most damning, was the fact that he didn't do good out of pure motives, but because he was terrified that if he didn't do good, he would be condemned. He thought that if he didn't do his absolute best, God would refuse to grant saving grace. This vexed the young professor, because it seemed that God had given humanity an impossible standard. How could anyone be at peace if God demanded so much from them? It is worth quoting Luther's own reflections at some length:

> I hated that word "the righteousness of God," which, according to the use and custom of all the teachers I had been taught to understand philosophically regarding the formal or active righteousness, as they called it, with which God is righteous and punishes the unrighteous sinner. Though I lived as a monk without reproach, I felt that I was a sinner before God with an extremely disturbed conscience. I could not believe that he was placated by my satisfaction. I did not love, yes I hated the righteous God who punishes sinners, and secretly, if not blasphemously, certainly murmuring greatly, I was angry with God and said, 'as if, indeed, it is not enough, that miserable sinners, eternally lost through original sin, are crushed by every kind of calamity … without having God add pain on pain by […] threatening us with his righteousness and wrath!' Thus I raged with a fierce and troubled conscience.[17]

Luther responded to his frustrations with a deeper study of the Bible. He studied Greek and Hebrew in order to better understand the meaning of the text. Above all, he was determined to discover something that could ease his troubled conscience and reconcile him with God. As early as his first lectures on the Psalms, his writings show him experimenting with different ways of looking at God's righteousness.[18] Rather than seeing righteousness merely as a standard to which God held sinners accountable, Luther began to understand righteousness as a gift that God gave to sinners. This new concept—which would eventually come to be known as *justification by faith alone*—would grow into the central focus of Luther's thought. Most of his later theology grew out of this simple idea.

There is a good deal of scholarly disagreement about precisely when and how Luther's view of God's grace began to change. It was once commonly held that Luther had already changed his thinking about grace and righteousness by 1513, when he began an important series of lectures on Romans. This view has lost favor, however, and some scholars now suggest that Luther did not fully change his ideas until after the indulgence controversy was well underway in 1517.[19] It seems clear, however, that this development in Luther's thinking did not happen suddenly, but was the gradual result of long study and reflection. Furthermore, it seems clear that even after he had begun to break away from the church, his understanding of the nature of salvation was still developing. In all probability, the pressure of his conflict with the church had the effect of crystalizing his theological ideas.

He reported that he had a particular breakthrough in 1518, when he was lecturing on Romans:

> At last, by the mercy of God, meditating day and night, I gave heed to the context of the words (Romans 1:17), namely, "in it the righteousness of God is revealed, as it is written, 'he who through faith is righteous shall live.'" There I began to understand that the righteousness of God is that by which the righteous lives by a gift of God, namely by faith. And this is the meaning: the righteousness of God is revealed by the gospel, namely, the passive righteousness with which merciful God justifies us by faith, as it is written, 'he who through faith is righteous shall live.' Here I felt that I was altogether born again and had entered paradise itself through open gates.[20]

This idea had at least one resounding implication for Luther. He did not need to obsess over his worthiness before God. Salvation was a gift, which God promised to all who would accept it. This was a joyful discovery for Luther, but it also cast a great deal of traditional medieval theology into question.

Chapter 3

THE ACCIDENTAL REFORMER

Despite the fact that he was developing a new and distinctive theology, until 1517, Luther remained a relatively minor figure—an undistinguished theology professor at a tiny university tucked away in Saxony. But this would soon change dramatically. Luther would be instantly, and unexpectedly, catapulted into the international spotlight and would, by 1520, be one of the most famous men in Europe.

3.1 The Indulgence Controversy

The act that launched Luther's career as a church reformer was relatively small—or at least it seemed to be at the time. As a university professor, one of Luther's duties was to engage occasionally in public debates—called disputations—about theological or philosophical topics. The professor would draft a series of theses that he would be willing to defend, post these theses publicly, and then take on whoever wanted to argue against him in a public debate. These debates were intended to clarify disputed issues, to deepen the intellect and rhetorical skills of participants, and to some degree to entertain and education the audience, which would typically be made up of university students. Proposing such a debate, even on a controversial topic, would have raised few eyebrows. So when, in 1517, Luther posted a list of theses critical of the church's teachings on indulgences, he did not expect to ignite a church-wide controversy.

3.1.1 What is an indulgence?

Luther's 95 *Theses* opposed the sale of indulgences.[1] These were an outgrowth of the sacrament of penance. Late medieval theology held that a person in a state of sin could not enter heaven. This was inconvenient because all people—even deeply religious ones—tended to continue to sin regularly. Fortunately, the church had a process by which sinners could return to a state of grace after sinning. The sinners must first repent and confess their sins to a priest. After this, sinners must perform some act of penance. Only after these steps had been accomplished could sin be atoned for and a sinner be reconciled to God. If a person died in a state of sin, without having performed the proper penance, he or she could not go directly to heaven. Instead, assuming that they were in all other respects faithful Christians, sinners who had not completed all of their penance would go to an intermediate place called purgatory, where they could complete the unresolved penance and cleanse themselves from sin before they were admitted to heaven. People in Luther's time generally believed purgatory to be a place of torment—very much like hell, only temporary. It was also assumed that all but the most saintly people would spend many years in purgatory before they fully atoned for all of their sins and entered the presence of God.

It is important to recognize that indulgences were essentially a remission of *penance*. They did not grant *forgiveness* of sins—this was accomplished by repentance and confession. Instead, they took the place of the acts of penance that the priest would assign after the confession. The church claimed the right to remit the penance associated with sins, and often did so in recognition of some particular act of merit. Often this would be something like going on a crusade or visiting shrines associated with the saints. Over time, though, the practice began to grow of offering remission of penance in exchange for a monetary donation to the church. The practice of exchanging indulgences for donations quickly grew, and soon overshadowed the earlier associations of indulgences with acts of merit. By 1517, indulgences were typically certificates, offered for sale by the church, which entitled the purchaser to the remission of some or all of their penance.

Indulgences were theologically dubious but very popular—both with the people, who saw them as a simple way to avoid the torments of purgatory, and with church officials for whom they could be a very effective fundraising device. They were also diametrically opposed to Luther's growing sense that God's grace was a free gift, and not contingent upon human efforts.

3.1.2 *Tetzel's plenary indulgence*

The particular incident that prompted the 95 *Theses* was the arrival in Germany of a traveling salesman by the name of John Tetzel. Tetzel was a Dominican friar who had made a career for himself as a successful seller of indulgences. He was an excellent salesman who knew how to close a deal.

His advance men arrived in town some weeks ahead of him to announce the forthcoming sale and to take stock of the townspeople's finances so that Tetzel could set his prices accordingly. Tetzel himself arrived later, with trumpet fanfare and colorful banners carrying the arms and insignia of the pope. He would then give a series of vivid sermons on the sufferings that awaited sinners in purgatory—but which could be avoided though the purchase of an indulgence. His sermons were designed to evoke an emotional response from the crowd. "Don't you hear the voices of your wailing dead parents and others who say 'have mercy upon me, have mercy upon me, because we are in severe punishment and pain,'" he would shout. "From this you could redeem us with a small [price] and yet you do not want to do so!"[2] He even had a catchy slogan—"when the coin in the coffer rings, the soul from purgatory springs!"

Tetzel had been authorized to offer a special plenary indulgence, which would cover all of the purchasers' sins—both those already committed and those yet to be committed. No sin was too abhorrent for this indulgence to absolve. It could be purchased on behalf of an already deceased friend or relative in order to release them immediately from purgatory. Furthermore, at least according to Tetzel's sales pitch, there was no need for actual repentance or for the sinner to change his or her ways. It was a simple financial transaction—buy the indulgence and your penance is completely covered. For many, this was a deal that was too good to pass up. Tetzel's sales soared.

Tetzel did not come to Wittenberg because Frederick the Wise—the ruler of Electoral Saxony and Luther's patron at the university—had banned him from all of his territories. Frederick himself had a large collection of relics which, when visited by a faithful penitent, carried their own indulgence, and he may not have wanted the competition. Tetzel did visit several nearby towns, though. Some of the faithful at Wittenberg bought indulgences from him, and Luther heard about his sales tactics. It seemed to Luther that this was an ideal opportunity to speak out about indulgences.

Luther had already written several times against the concept of indulgences.[3] He felt that they misled the faithful into believing that there was no need to repent from sins or to change their ways. Furthermore, Tetzel's over-the-top claims and slick sales tactics convinced Luther that Tetzel was a con-man defrauding the faithful. He hoped that, once Tetzel was brought to the attention of church officials, his license to sell would be revoked. Luther thus responded to Tetzel in the way that a sixteenth-century professor was expected to—he wrote and posted the 95 *Theses*.

Despite popular perception, this was not an act of defiance on Luther's part. The image of an angry Luther nailing his grievances to the church door is pure myth. He was legitimately critical of indulgences, but his goal in the 95 *Theses* was limited to pointing out abuses and was directed towards his fellow academics and not to the general public. His skepticism about indulgences was also not unique. Many theologians questioned the theological foundations of the practice. German noblemen also tended to resent the fact that money flowed out of Germany into the papal treasury as a result of indulgence sales. Humanists saw indulgences as evidence of the corruption and worldliness of the church. So Luther was in good company in critiquing the practice. Nor was he intentionally stirring up controversy. For Luther, posting the 95 *Theses* was very much like a modern college professor publishing an article in a scholarly journal. A public statement of opposition, to be sure, but hardly something that was likely to capture the attention of anybody beyond his small academic circle.

3.1.3 Did Luther actually post the 95 Theses?

Tradition holds that Luther nailed the 95 *Theses* to the door of the Castle Church in Wittenberg on October 31, 1517. The church door often served as a kind of community bulletin board, and Luther's theses were intended to announce a public debate. October 31 was a significant date because the following day was the feast of All Saints, so Luther could expect that most of the community would come to church and see the notice.

Recent scholarship has cast into doubt whether Luther actually nailed the theses to the door.[4] Luther himself never mentions actually posting the theses, and the public disputation that they were supposed to announce never took place. The first mention of Luther publicly posting the theses was made by his friend and biographer Philip Melanchthon—a man who will shortly become one of Luther's key associates. But Melanchthon was not present in Wittenberg during 1517, so he could not have been an eyewitness to the posting of the theses. And Melanchthon's biography was published after Luther's death and more than thirty years after the 95 *Theses*. Such arguments are far from conclusive, but they cast considerable doubt on the traditional story. What is certain, however, is that Luther drafted the theses and sent a copy of them, along with a polite cover letter, to his bishop, Albert of Mainz.

3.1.4 Power politics

With this letter to Albert, Luther inadvertently stepped into a sensitive situation. Tetzel's indulgence was no ordinary fundraiser. It was the outcome of a delicate financial arrangement between Albert and the pope. When Luther's letter arrived, Albert saw in it a potentially serious threat to his position and immediately forwarded it to the pope, who was as deeply involved with the indulgence as was Albert.

The indulgence had begun with Pope Leo X. Leo was a fairly typical renaissance pope. A member of the wealthy and influential Medici banking dynasty of Florence, he had been elevated to the papacy largely due to the influence of his powerful relatives. He was deeply embroiled in international politics and was often at war with neighboring Italian city-states. He wanted to increase the prestige of the papacy and sought to do so by renovating St. Peter's Basilica in Rome, which he intended to make the grandest church in Christendom. This was a magnificent idea, except for the fact that Leo was up to his eyeballs in debt and the renovations that he was planning were quite expensive. What he needed more than anything was a new source of income.

Albert was also in a delicate financial situation. He already held two church offices, as the Archbishop of both Magdeburg and Halberstadt. This was technically against church law, but such irregularities could usually be resolved by a donation to the pope. When the Archbishop of Mainz died in 1517, Albert saw the vacant position as a great opportunity. The see of Mainz was the leading ecclesiastical office in all of Germany, and its archbishop was one of the seven electors who chose the Holy Roman Emperor. It was a powerful position, and Albert wanted it. In order to obtain a third bishopric, though, he would need to make a very large donation to the pope to secure the necessary exemptions from church law. This was the opportunity that Leo had been looking for. The donation from Albert would go a long way toward defraying the costs of a new St. Peter's. Albert agreed to pay and took out a massive loan to cover the cost. Leo, in turn, authorized a special indulgence to be sold in Albert's territories, the proceeds of which would be split between Leo and Albert. Albert would use his share of the indulgence money to repay his loan and Leo would use his to finance his building project. This was the indulgence Tetzel was selling. Thus Luther's criticism of this particular indulgence was a matter far more serious than he had originally anticipated.

The *95 Theses* was a particularly effective criticism of the concept of indulgences, which is perhaps why Albert saw it as such a potential threat. In addition to drawing attention to the worldliness and corruption that were associated with indulgences, they also attacked the very theological foundations upon which the concept of indulgences was built. Taken as a whole, they formed a devastating critique, not only of Tetzel's indulgence, but of the entire system of penance of which indulgences were a part. The following selections will give a sense of the tone and character of the *95 Theses*:

> 6. The pope cannot remit any guilt, except by declaring and showing that it has [already] been remitted by God …

> 36. Any truly repentant Christian has a right to full remission of penalty and guilt, even without indulgence letters.
>
> 45. Christians ought to be taught that he who sees a needy man and passes him by, yet gives money for indulgences, does not buy papal indulgences but God's wrath.
>
> 82. ... why does not the pope empty purgatory for the sake of holy love and the dire need of the souls that are there if he redeems an infinite number of souls for the sake of miserable money with which to build a church? The former reasons would be just; the latter is most trivial.[5]

Luther apparently did not know of Albert's involvement in the marketing of the indulgence. He assumed that Tetzel was overstepping his authority in making such grandiose claims about the power of indulgences. He hoped that, once Albert's attention had been drawn to Tetzel's abuses, he would put a stop to the indulgence trade. Instead, by threatening one of Albert's important sources of income, Luther had ignited a firestorm that would soon draw the attention of the most powerful men in Europe.

Leo, upon receiving Luther's letter from Albert, did not respond immediately. Perhaps he hoped that the whole affair would quickly blow over. It did not. Although Luther addressed the 95 *Theses* to a small, academic audience, they quickly began to circulate much more broadly. The printing press, the state-of-the-art information technology of its day, made it possible for written works to spread much more quickly than ever before. Some of Luther's friends, apparently without Luther's knowledge, had the 95 *Theses* printed and distributed. They proved very popular. By the end of 1517, printed copies of the 95 *Theses* were being circulated in several important German cities. Soon, they were translated from Luther's original Latin—a language only accessible to a well-educated minority—into German. Then they began to circulate among the middle and lower classes as well. By March 1518, they had reached the celebrated humanists Erasmus and Thomas More.[6] Once they had spread so widely, there was no way for the pope to quietly contain the situation. It was clear that Leo would have to respond publicly in some way.

Leo initially handed the Luther case over to Luther's own Augustinian order, asking that Luther be disciplined for spreading new ideas and for interfering with Tetzel's indulgence sales. Responsibility for disciplining Luther passed down to Staupitz, Luther's friend and confessor, who did not pursue the matter. At the same time, forces in Rome began to push for a more vigorous response. Several prominent members of the papal curia saw in Luther's critique of indulgences a deeper attack on papal primacy and scholastic theology. It seems likely, given the nature of their response, that they may have suspected Luther of supporting conciliarism, which the papacy had spent 100 years trying to eradicate.

So Leo handed Luther's letter over to Sylvester Mazzolini, known as Prierias, whom he assigned to begin disciplinary processes against Luther. Prierias was a highly placed papal advisor and a staunch advocate of papal power. Like Tetzel, he was a Dominican. The Dominicans were often rivals to Luther's Augustinian order, so the appointment of Prierias as Luther's judge was not sympathetic to Luther. Prierias wrote a response to the 95 Theses carrying the rather unwieldy title *Dialogue Against the Arrogant Theses of Martin Luther Concerning the Power of the Pope*. In it, he did not address Luther's doctrinal assertions about the need for repentance or the role of faith in salvation. Instead, he accused Luther of heresy based solely on the fact that he questioned the teaching of the pope. "The pope cannot err," he claimed, "when he in his capacity as pope comes to a decision… he who does not hold to the teachings of the Roman Church and the pope as an infallible rule of faith, from which even the Holy Scripture draws its power and authority, is a heretic."[7]

Prierias' heavy-handed defense of the pope did not impress Luther. It arrived at Wittenberg along with a summons to appear personally in Rome to defend himself against a charge of heresy. The vigor of the response must have impressed Luther, who was only now beginning to realize what sort of hornet's nest he had wandered into. He thought Prierias' treatise to be so poorly reasoned that it hardly merited a response, though. He later recalled his reaction upon receiving the summons to Rome: "Then I thought, 'Good God, has it come to this that the matter will go before the pope?' However, our Lord God was gracious to me, and the stupid dolt wrote such wretched stuff that I had to laugh."[8] He did ultimately compose a reply, though, that marshaled arguments from scripture and the church fathers to insist that the pope could, in fact, err.

Luther had not intended to challenge the authority of the pope, nor did he want to start a revolution. He was critical of indulgences, but only because he saw them as an impediment to the true Catholic faith. But the 95 Theses were, in fact, more than an attack on a specific, if particularly egregious, example of corruption. They reflected a more thoroughgoing rethinking of the theology that he had been taught, in light of the deep study of the Bible he had been engaged in. The arguments that he made in the 95 Theses, when taken to their logical conclusion, raised important questions about the nature of the sacraments, the forgiveness of sins, and the role of the pope. Prierias recognized this, and saw in Luther a potentially powerful challenge to papal authority. It is not clear, however, that Luther fully understood the implications of the line of thought that started with the 95 Theses. It would take the events of the next two years for him to recognize that he was, in fact, breaking with the church.

3.2 The Heidelberg Disputation

Luther's first major public appearance after the publication of the *95 Theses* was at the triennial meeting of the Augustinian Order. This meeting was to be held in the city of Heidelberg, and Luther was attending as a part of his duties as a district vicar within the order. He was also scheduled to be the main speaker in a public disputation, which was a traditional feature of these meetings. Because of the *95 Theses*, Luther was something of a minor celebrity, and many of the assembled monks expected that he would take up the question of indulgences in his disputation. Instead, Luther used the opportunity to present a much broader case against scholastic theology.

Although the assembled Augustinians were expected to be a generally friendly audience for Luther, he was still suspected of heresy, and some of his friends worried about his safety when he travelled the 300 miles from Wittenberg to Heidelberg. Cautiously, he set out on foot on April 11, 1518. He was accompanied by one fellow friar, and later met up with a group of Augustinians travelling from Erfurt, who were likely known to Luther from his time there. They arrived at Heidelberg without incident, several days before the meeting was to start.

At Heidelberg, Luther first presented the main points of what would eventually become Protestant theology. Human beings, he argued, can do nothing to save themselves. Our noblest actions are still tainted by sinful motives, because we ultimately love ourselves more than we love God. No human effort, no sacrament, can change this foundational fact. Seeking to reconcile ourselves with God through our own efforts is doomed to fail, which is why indulgences cannot help us. Rather than seeking salvation through our own efforts and actions, Luther continued, Christians should look to the suffering and ignominy of Jesus on the cross. We cannot save ourselves, and any theology that claims that human effort can reconcile us with God is not only false, but dangerous. Our only hope is to fall upon God's mercy. He concluded his remarks on a hopeful note:

> Therefore it is the sweetest righteousness of God the Father that he does not save imaginary, but rather, real sinners, sustaining us in spite of our sins and accepting our works and lives which are all deserving of rejection, until he perfects and saves us. Meanwhile, we live under the protection and the shadow of his wings and escape judgment through his mercy, not through our righteousness.[9]

Scholastic theology, or as Luther termed it, "the theology of glory," focused on human wisdom and achievement and, as such, could never reconcile sinners with God. On the other hand, a "theology of the cross" that focused on Christ's suffering is the true path to grace. "It is certain," he wrote, "that a man must completely despair of himself in order to become fit to obtain the grace of Christ."[10] Luther insisted that salvation can only be God's achievement, and that humans need only faithfully accept God's gift.[11]

Not all of the theologians gathered at Heidelberg agreed with Luther's conclusions, but many did. Martin Bucer, a young Dominican who had attended the meeting as an observer was won over by Luther's arguments. Bucer brought Luther's theology back to his native Strasbourg, where he would become an important Protestant leader. He wrote to a friend that Luther's "sweetness in answering is remarkable, his patience in listening is incomparable, in his explanations you would recognize the acumen of St. Paul... his answers, so brief, so wise, and drawn from the Holy Scriptures, easily made all of his hearers his admirers."[12] Luther gained many admirers like Bucer—enough so that he left the meeting with high hopes that, even though the older, more traditional theologians rejected him, the younger generation might embrace his theology. Upon his return to Wittenberg, he wrote to his friend, the Elector's secretary George Spalatin, "I have great hope that ... this true theology ... rejected by those opinionated old men, will pass over to the younger generation."[13]

3.3 Friends in High Places

Despite Luther's hopes for the younger generation, supporters of the pope were still determined to stop Luther. Irate that Luther had interfered with his profits, Tetzel wrote diatribes against Luther throughout 1518, mostly emphasizing the absolute power of the pope. But Tetzel was not a good scholar, and Luther mostly ignored his writings. More substantial Catholic scholars began to take notice of the brewing controversy surrounding Luther, though. Luther would soon find himself debating not just indulgence peddlers like Tetzel, but some of Europe's most celebrated theological minds.

Luther had been summoned to appear before a church court in Rome to defend himself against charges of heresy. This was a dangerous situation, and Luther knew it. He might have reflected on the case of Jan Hus, the Bohemian priest and follower of Wyclif who in 1415 had been summoned to the Council of Constance to defend himself against similar charges of heresy. Despite a promise of safe conduct issued by the Emperor, Hus was burned at the stake when he refused to recant. Luther knew that the stakes were just as high in his case. Unlike Hus, however, Luther had some distinct political advantages.

The chief of these advantages was that Luther's prince, Elector Frederick the Wise of Saxony, was willing to protect Luther. Frederick, like many German princes of his era, resented papal interference in German politics. Furthermore, he was jealously protective of the university he had founded in Wittenberg and was not about to let the pope take away his star professor. Frederick was also one of the seven electors, who had the privilege of choosing the Holy Roman Emperors. This position gave Frederick a substantial amount of influence in 1518 because the Emperor Maximilian was growing old, and it was clear that an imperial election would be held within the next several years. The leading candidate for the imperial office was Maximilian's grandson, Charles of Spain. Charles already ruled Spain, Burgundy, Naples, and Austria. The pope feared that if Charles were also given the imperial title, he would become far too powerful. Leo saw Frederick as a potential rival candidate for the imperial throne, and even if Frederick were not willing to take the title himself, he might be convinced to throw his support behind another alternative candidate. It was therefore important that the pope maintain good relations with Frederick. Thus, Leo was moved cautiously with regard to Luther, in order not to alienate Frederick.

When Luther received his summons to Rome, he appealed to Frederick. He could not expect a fair trial in Rome, and feared for his safety. Frederick intervened and convinced Leo to transfer Luther's examination to the German city of Augsburg, where an Imperial Diet—the regular meeting of the German princes—was to occur in October of 1518. Cardinal Cajetan, the papal legate to the Diet, would be in Augsburg anyway, and Leo ordered Cajetan to examine Luther. Cajetan was authorized to offer clemency to Luther if he should recant—but also to arrest him and bring him to Rome should he refuse to recant. So Luther's trial would be held on German soil.

Unlike Tetzel and Prierias, Cajetan was a fair-minded scholar who seemed determined to give Luther fair treatment. He studied the issues carefully, reading all of Luther's relevant writings. But he was also under strict orders not to allow Luther to debate the issues. He must either extract a recantation from Luther or have him arrested.

Setting out for Augsburg, Luther knew that his life was in danger. He knew that, like Hus, his journey might end at the stake. "What a shame I have become to my parents," he mourned.[14] His friends urged him to take great care in his interview with Cajetan, and worked behind the scenes to arrange for him safe lodging and travel within Augsburg.

Luther appeared at Augsburg on October 7, 1518, but was not able to have his interview with Cajetan until October 12. At the interview, Cajetan tried to avoid discussing theology with Luther. He simply instructed Luther to repent of his errors, to promise not to teach them again, and to refrain from disturbing the peace of the church. But Luther was not willing to give up without a fight. He refused to recant without being specifically shown the error of his ways. For the next three days, Cajetan tried vainly to convince Luther to recant and admit to having been in error. Luther, on the other hand, strove to engage the cardinal in a debate about doctrine. Ultimately the issue that separated the two men was the question of religious authority. As had Prierias, Cajetan insisted that the Pope's authority was absolute and final. Papal authority gave the church order and structure, without which things could easily descend into chaos. In Cajetan's opinion, Luther—because he refused to accept the pope's judgment that he was in error—was by that very fact a heretic. Luther countered Cajetan's defense of papal authority by insisting that even the pope was subject to the Bible. He amassed evidence from the Bible, as well as from church fathers such as Bernard of Clairvaux, to support his position that sinners were justified by their faith alone, and not through the power of the church. Since, for Luther, the Bible's authority trumped that of the pope, he could not accept the pope's charge of heresy. "As long as these Scripture passages stand," he claimed, "I cannot [recant], for I know that one must obey God rather than men."[15]

The cardinal was furious, and ended the hearing after three days, frustrated at Luther's obstinate refusal to recant. Luther was ecstatic, and wrote to his friend and fellow Wittenberg professor Andreas Karlstadt that Cajetan's confidence was shattered. He recognized that it would have been the easiest thing in the world to recant, but had refused to do so because he was convinced that he was right. In his letter to Karlstadt, he described the situation: "I knew that I would be the most agreeable and dearest of all, if only I would say this one word: '*revoco*,' that is, 'I recant.' But I won't make myself a heretic by contradicting the opinion which made me a Christian. I will die first by fire, or be exiled and cursed."[16]

By refusing to recant, and by goading Cajetan into a debate about papal authority, Luther knew that he was almost certain to be excommunicated. He was also flirting with death at the stake as a heretic. He consulted his friends and advisors. Upon their advice, he decided upon a daring course of action. He sent a written appeal to the pope himself. In the appeal, Luther outlined his position, and suggested that Cajetan and the other Dominicans who had stood in judgment of his writings had not been impartial because of the long-standing rivalry between the Dominicans and the Augustinians. He pledged his submission, and announced his readiness to hear Leo's judgment.

After sending the letter, and fearing that he would soon be arrested, Luther fled Augsburg in the middle of the night. Returning to the relative safety of Wittenberg, he penned a second, more defiant appeal. This time, Luther appealed not to the pope, but to a church council. There was some precedent for this, but Pope Pius II had explicitly condemned such an appeal in 1460 during the conflict with the conciliarists. Such an appeal more closely associated Luther with the conciliarists in his enemies' estimation. Such an appeal was a forthright defiance of papal authority, and pitted Luther directly against the pope and all of the power of the papacy.

3.4 The Leipzig Debate

The Emperor Maximilian died in January of 1519. The election of a new emperor soon became the most important issue in Germany. Pope Leo opposed the ambitions of the Habsburg family, who had held the imperial throne since 1440. He wanted a non-Habsburg emperor and was trying desperately to curry favor with the electors. This was a fortunate political situation for Luther.

Because of the vacant imperial throne, Luther didn't need to worry about arrest or persecution from imperial authorities for the time being. Since the attention of the papacy was focused on the forthcoming imperial election, the question of Luther's heresy had suddenly become a much lower priority. Perhaps most importantly, the election dramatically increased the power and influence of Luther's prince and protector, Frederick the Wise. Frederick's vote was coveted by the pope, who hoped to convince Frederick to throw his support to an alternative candidate. And Frederick did not want to have Luther harmed. For the time being, he got his way. The pope would rather have Frederick's support in the imperial election than have Luther silenced.

So Luther was free to go about his typical academic duties throughout early 1519: teaching classes, writing treatises, preaching sermons and studying. He worked on his Greek and Hebrew in order to better understand the Bible. His written exchanges with Prierias and his encounter with Cajetan had left him convinced that the papacy stood in direct opposition to scripture, but had yet to decisively break from the church. All the same, it was beginning to look very unlikely that Luther would ever reconcile with the church. At least not without the church undergoing a thorough reformation.

The doctrinal issues that Luther had raised in the 95 *Theses* and at the Heidelberg disputation had not been resolved. Luther's friend and fellow Wittenberg professor Andreas Karlstadt had been won over to Luther's developing Protestant theology, and had been engaged in a furious written debate with the Catholic theologian Johannes Eck of the University of Ingolstadt—one of the leading theologians of the day. Karlstadt supported Luther's positions on papal authority and the effectiveness of indulgences, while Eck defended the papacy. Eck challenged Karlstadt to a public debate, hoping that Luther would also attend. Duke George of Saxony, Frederick the Wise's cousin and rival, provided a venue for the debate at the University of Leipzig. Leipzig, which was outside of Frederick's Electoral Saxony, was not a favorable site for Luther. The Leipzig faculty was sympathetic to the papacy, and it would be difficult for Frederick to protect Luther if he left Frederick's territory. Luther was also well aware that further public disputes could be dangerous to his reputation and to his safety. Nevertheless, the opportunity to debate Eck was too good to pass up.

So Karlstadt accepted Eck's challenge. In early June, he set out for Leipzig, taking with him Luther and some 200 armed students. Clearly, they saw that this might be something more than a friendly discussion. Luther was still suspected of heresy, and rumors abounded of potential assassination attempts.

The entourage arrived at Leipzig without incident. There they were warmly welcomed and feted at a grand banquet. The university community was excited to hear some of Europe's most noteworthy theologians debate some of the hottest issues of the day. There was a festive, exciting atmosphere surrounding the debate. Eck had something of a home-field advantage, as he was supported by the theological faculty from Leipzig, but supporters of Luther had travelled from Erfurt and Zwickau to support Karlstadt.

The debate began with Karlstadt and Eck as the main disputants. It was quickly clear that Eck was the better orator. His quick mind and extensive memory served him well. Karlstadt, on the other hand, relied heavily on his books and notes and seemed to be unsure of himself. Eck challenged Karlstadt to set aside his books and rely on his memory alone, as was the typical custom for academic disputations. Without his books, Karlstadt began to flounder and could not continue. Luther stepped up to support his colleague. This is almost certainly what Eck wanted.

Luther was a better debater than Karlstadt, and certainly a bigger celebrity. Eck immediately steered the debate to the issue of papal authority. Luther repeated the arguments that he had already presented to Cajetan. The true head of the church, he claimed, was Christ and not the pope. He supported his arguments with references to scripture and citations from the early church fathers. The tables began to turn and now Eck was on the defensive. But Eck was not finished yet. He claimed that by refusing to accept the authority of the pope, Luther must be in agreement with Hus, who had been authoritatively condemned in 1415. Hus' arguments were indeed similar to Luther's. He had also claimed that Christ—not the pope—was the true head of the church.

The connection with Hus was serious, and Luther knew it. At first he tried to deny that he was in agreement with Hus, but later, during a break in the proceedings, Luther read up on what Hus had taught and found that he did, indeed, agree with Hus on several points. The next day, under pressure from Eck, Luther admitted that he agreed in some ways with Hus, and suggested that the Council of Constance had erred in condemning Hus. This was very significant. Luther had now not only questioned the authority of the pope, but also that of church councils. The only authority that Luther would admit was that of the Bible.

He concluded his remarks at Leipzig with the comment, "I grieve that the Holy Doctor [Eck] penetrates the scripture as profoundly as a water spider the water, in fact, he flees from them as the devil from the cross."[17]

The debate dragged on for three weeks without reaching any conclusion. Eventually, Duke George called it to a halt. He was expecting important guests and wanted to clear out the unruly crowds before they arrived. The debate had soured him on Luther, and he remained an implacable opponent of the reformation for the rest of his life. There was no conclusive victor, although both sides proclaimed themselves to have won. The Leipzig debate had left a lasting mark, though. It crystallized some of the issues involved in Luther's conflict with the church—specifically the potential connections between Luther and Hus. It also illustrated to the watching world that the chasm between Luther and the papacy was too wide to be easily healed.

3.5   1520: The Decisive Year

After Leipzig, Luther's position was clear. In 1517, he had been a loyal son of the church. His criticism of indulgences had grown out of a pastor's concern for the spiritual life of his congregation, and had been developed in hopes that the church would accept his critique and move toward reform. But during his debates with Prierias, Cajetan and Eck he had encountered church officials who were unwilling to compromise. Where Luther sought reasoned arguments, he found instead the bald assertion of raw papal power. Luther was disappointed that these theologians were either unwilling or unable to read the Bible deeply and began to conclude that the Catholic Church was in fact an impediment to the true gospel.

3.5.1   *Excommunication*

Until 1519, despite his defiance of church authorities, the papacy had been unwilling or unable to pursue Luther with any sort of vigor. Frederick was still a key vote in the imperial election and Pope Leo still held out hope that Frederick would support a pro-papal candidate. Shortages in the papal finances and the military threat to southern Europe posed by the Turks also loomed larger in Leo's mind than German theological disputes.

By 1520, however, the situation had changed. Charles of Spain had been elected Holy Roman Emperor on June 28, 1519, as Luther and Eck were debating at Leipzig. Leo's hope for a non-Habsburg emperor was thwarted, and Frederick's goodwill was no longer as vital for the pope as it had been the previous year. Furthermore, the delay in acting against Luther had only served to increase Luther's popularity. So Leo couldn't hesitate any longer. A commission was established in Rome to decide what to do about Luther. Its members included both Cajetan and Eck. The commission determined that Luther's teachings were heretical, and that his refusal to recant was further evidence of his defiance of legitimate papal authority. On June 24, 1520, the commission drafted a bull of excommunication—named *Exsurge Domine* after its opening words in Latin. The bull gave Luther 60 days to recant of his heresy. At the end of 60 days, if he had not formally recanted, Luther would be considered to have been excommunicated.

True to form, Luther refused to recant, even under the threat of excommunication. Instead, he was stubbornly defiant. In late June, Eck and the papal ambassador Jerome Aleander began to promulgate the bull of excommunication in Germany. Typically the public announcement of the excommunication of a heretic included public burnings of the condemned heretic's books, and Eck and Aleander arranged several bonfires to which they consigned Luther's books. In Wittenberg, Luther responded with his own burning. On December 10, accompanied by supportive students and colleagues from the university, Luther publicly burned not only the bull of excommunication, but also books of church law, papal pronouncements, and works of scholastic theology. The excommunication and Luther's defiant reaction to it marked the final break between Luther and the church. His excommunication was finalized on January 3, 1521, after which Luther was officially considered to be a heretic. He would never reconcile with the church.

3.5.2 *Political support for Luther*

His growing break with church authorities cost Luther some popular support, but Frederick the Wise still protected him. Most of his colleagues and students at Wittenberg were on his side, so he was able to continue his academic duties with little interruption. Luther also remained popular with many of the German nobles, who saw his split with the church as a potential tool in their own conflicts with both the papacy and the emperor. Ulrich von Hutten, a German nobleman and well-known humanist wrote to Luther's friend and colleague Philip Melanchthon in early 1520 offering support and military assistance for Luther in his conflict with the pope.[18] Several months later, he wrote an open letter to all Germans, which illustrates the political overtones that surrounded the German nobility's support for Luther:

> Behold, men of Germany, the bull of Leo X by which he tries to suppress the rising truth of Christianity, which he opposes to our liberty, lest, after her long bondage she should again grow strong and revive. Shall we not resist him in this attempt, and take public counsel lest he should go farther and before we know it accomplish something for his insatiable cupidity and impudence? ... Luther is not touched in this, but all of us; nor is the sword drawn against one only, but we are all threatened. They will never complain of his tyranny, never uncover his fraud, never lay bare his guile nor resist his fury nor impede his robbery... remember to act like Germans.[19]

Hutten's letter indicates the degree to which Luther's theology was becoming conflated with German nationalism. Hutten clearly believed that there was a strong connection between Luther's theology and German political freedom. In this, he was far from alone.

Knowing that, as an excommunicated heretic, his life was in jeopardy, and fearing assassination and arrest, Luther worked tirelessly throughout 1520, devoting much of his time to writing. He composed dozens of treatises on many subjects throughout the year, and all were quickly printed and circulated widely in Europe. Luther had a gift for lucid, direct writing, and non-scholars found his writings accessible and compelling. Many of his writings were composed in German, or were quickly translated into German and were therefore available to the reading public instead of limited to those with knowledge of the scholarly language of Latin. Luther's fame grew as each new treatise was printed. He was a celebrity, and his popularity in Germany skyrocketed. The papacy could not keep up. The Catholic writers who opposed Luther did not have Luther's charisma or flair for speaking to the people in their own language. Nor were they able to capture the people's imagination as did Luther. So, despite his excommunication, Luther was beginning to emerge as a kind of German folk hero.

3.5.3 The key writings of 1520

Of Luther's dozens of writings, three small treatises, all published in the fall of 1520, are the most significant. *The Address to the Christian Nobility*, *The Babylonian Captivity of the Church*, and *The Freedom of A Christian* have been called the central writings of the reformation. Any serious student of Luther really ought to read them all in their entirety. They are relatively brief, widely available in English translations and give a vibrant picture of the reformer in his prime. The three treatises together describe the key theological positions that Luther would defend for the rest of his career.

The first of these key treatises, *The Address to the Christian Nobility*, was published in German and addressed directly to the political authorities of the Holy Roman Empire.[20] In it, Luther proposed a thoroughgoing reform of the church. Many German nobles, like von Hutten, had been calling for such a reform for years. The problem, Luther suggested, was that the church would never actually reform itself from the inside. It had barricaded itself behind a series of walls designed to protect its own power and to avoid any sort of reform. The only option, Luther claimed, was for the German princes to wrest power from the church hierarchy and make the needed reforms for themselves. Since the princes have been commissioned by God to promote their citizens' welfare, it is their religious duty to oppose a church that defied the true gospel. He wrote:

> Therefore, when necessity demands it and the pope is an offense to Christendom, the first man who is able should, as a true member of the body, do what he can to bring about a truly free council. No one can do this as well as the temporal authorities... Whenever it is necessary or profitable they ought to exercise the office and work which they have received from God over everyone.[21]

This was a call to the secular authorities in Germany to join him in his break with the church. He called upon the princes to seize power from the church and to implement reforms on their own authority. This appealed to many German princes who might otherwise disagree with Luther's theology. It also demonstrated something about Luther's own distinctive political views. Luther saw secular government as divinely ordained and as an alternate source of religious authority to the corrupt Catholic Church. He urged secular rulers to act decisively and to understand that their actions bore the stamp of divine approval.

Luther knew that this tract was going to be deeply controversial; it was, after all, a direct attack on the Roman church. But he was not willing to back down when he believed himself to be right. He wrote about the *Address to the Christian Nobility* in a letter to Spalatin on August 5. In the letter he is clearly aware that the treatise would cause a storm, but insists that it is a "necessary attack on the tyranny of the Roman Antichrist who destroys the souls of the whole world ... I hope it will make even those languid little evil-seekers gasp."[22] He went on to imply that he had something even more irritating for the pope up his sleeve.

This irritating treatise, *The Babylonian Captivity of the Church*, was both more theological and more controversial than the *Address to the Christian Nobility*.[23] Unlike the earlier treatise, this one was written in Latin, intended for a scholarly audience. In it, Luther challenged the church's teachings on the sacraments. Luther's conviction that salvation was by faith and not through human action was bound to prompt him to think deeply about the role and nature of the sacraments, which were central to the church's teachings on salvation.

The title is a metaphor. Just as the Hebrews in the Old Testament were carried off into captivity in Babylon, so now, Luther claimed, were the sacraments of the church held captive by the papacy. His readers would also certainly have recognized that "Babylon" was also a symbol of the antichrist in the book of Revelation, and they would have understood Luther's implication that the pope was a kind of antichrist.

Luther begins by reducing the number of the sacraments from seven to three. He retained only baptism, the Eucharist and penance. He would eventually even talk himself out of penance as a sacrament, leaving only the first two. Confession and penance, he ultimately decided, were ways to renew the vows made at baptism, and were thus a part of the larger sacrament of baptism.

The most important part of the treatise is Luther's treatment of the Eucharist. This sacrament, he claims, has been taken captive by the church, which uses its control over it to enhance its own power. He is critical of the common practice of reserving the wine of the sacrament for the clergy–laypeople received only the bread. For Luther, this was simply tyranny, and marked an artificial distinction between clergy and laity. He also questioned the traditional doctrine of transubstantiation, in which the bread and wine mystically become Jesus' real body and blood. Luther continued to believe that Jesus was truly, physically present in the bread and wine of the Eucharist, but insisted that the church could not condemn anyone as a heretic for simply refusing to consent to what he saw as an abstract philosophical argument.

What made the *Babylonian Captivity* so deeply controversial, though, was Luther's redefinition of what a sacrament was. The church taught that the sacraments were, in a sense, automatically effective. That is, the power of reconciling sinners to God is somehow present within the sacrament, and will work to reconcile anybody who partakes in the sacrament. For Luther, this made the sacraments into a human act by which we can try to earn our own salvation. His alternate definition held that the sacraments were not effective in and of themselves, but were dependent upon a person receiving the sacraments in faith. It was the faith that effected reconciliation with God—not the sacrament.

What is particularly interesting here is the way that Luther continues to maintain a deep respect for the sacraments. More radical reformers would later reject the idea that Christ was truly present in the sacraments, but Luther doggedly held to this idea. The Eucharist and baptism were, for Luther, real and effective—but it was not the physical elements themselves—bread, wine and water—that were effective, but the faith of the recipient in the word of God. Luther seems to have seen the sacraments themselves as a tangible sign of God's promise—something like a wedding ring is a tangible sign of the promises made by a bride and groom.[24]

It was this wholesale upending of traditional sacramental theology that made *The Babylonian Captivity* what Heinrich Boehmer calls the "most radical of Luther's writings."[25] Johannes Bugenhagen, who would later become one of Luther's most devoted followers, was aghast when he first read the treatise, and considered Luther to be the worst possible heretic. But after another, more careful, reading, Bugenhagen changed his mind. "The whole world is blind as can be," he said, "but this is the one man who sees the truth."[26] Others were not so sympathetic. King Henry VIII of England was so offended by Luther's attack on the sacraments that he composed a tract of his own to defend the sacraments. Henry's *Defense of the Seven Sacraments* so impressed Pope Leo that he rewarded Henry with the title "defender of the faith."

The *Babylonian Captivity* and the *Address to the Christian Nobility* were each overt assaults on the church, but even as Luther was publishing them, a few still held out hope that Luther would reconcile with the pope. Karl von Miltitz, the papal ambassador to the court of Frederick the Wise, took it upon himself to negotiate with Luther. He convinced Luther to write a letter to the pope, in which he would politely defend his theology. This letter developed into the tract *On the Freedom of a Christian*.[27] In it, Luther summarized the central features of his theology and sketched out some of its practical consequences.

Unlike the first two treatises, *On the Freedom of a Christian* was written in an irenic tone. In it, Luther does not directly attack the church, but presents what he felt to be the central elements of the gospel. In the opening line he presents a seeming contradiction: "A Christian," he says, "is a perfectly free lord of all, subject to none." On the other hand, "a Christian is a perfectly dutiful servant of all, subject to all."[28] He granted that these seem to contradict one another, but went on to explain that they described two distinct, but complimentary aspects of the Christian life.

His argument begins with justification by faith: "It is evident that no external thing has any influence in producing Christian righteousness or freedom, or in producing unrighteousness or servitude."[29] Our actions cannot help us to reconcile with God, in other words, but neither can they condemn us. Luther felt that Christ has made us righteous through his death on the cross—and human actions are completely irrelevant to this simple fact. So, in this sense, Christians are free. As long as we have faith in Christ, Luther thought, we do not have to be subject to external requirements in order to earn God's pleasure.

This spiritual freedom, however, should not be interpreted as license to behave indulgently. Instead, Luther argues, the spiritual freedom that comes from justification by faith transforms the believer, so that she will continue to do good works—not to become holier or more Christian, but out of gratitude for what God has done for her and out of love for her neighbors. He concludes with an exhortation not to reject good works, but to understand that only faith in Christ would save:

> Our faith in Christ does not free us from works but from false opinions concerning works, that is, from the foolish presumption that justification is acquired by works [...] Thus what we do, live, and are in works and ceremonies we do because of the necessities of this life and of the effort to rule our body. Nevertheless, we are justified not in these but in the faith of the Son of God.[30]

The *Freedom of a Christian* addresses one of the most important questions raised by Luther's teaching. If, as Luther asserted, we are saved by faith in Christ, regardless of our actions, what reason to we then have to act morally? Luther's solution is elegant, but philosophically complex. Many of Luther's followers heard him say that Christians were free and not subject to any external laws, and understood this to mean that Luther endorsed political rebellion or a wholesale rejection of traditional morality. *The Freedom of a Christian* makes it clear that Luther did not understand freedom in those terms, though.

3.6 The Diet of Worms

The events of 1520 made it crystal clear that Luther had broken away from the church, and that he was unwilling to compromise any of his new theology in order to reconcile with the church. He had been officially excommunicated, and would certainly be executed as a heretic if the church were to get its hands on him. But Luther still had a good deal of support, both from the German public and from some influential political figures as well. He was in no immediate danger—so long as the secular authorities in Saxony didn't decide to turn him over to Rome. In Wittenberg, Frederick the Wise continued to shelter Luther from the pope, but he was now facing increasing pressure, both from church representatives and from the newly elected emperor, Charles V.

Charles was in a delicate position. He was a pious man and anxious to do what God wanted. But he also recognized that Pope Leo had opposed his election as emperor, and was thus not willing to simply do as the pope told him. In addition to this, he needed to maintain the support and goodwill of the German princes if he were to govern the empire with any sort of effectiveness. So, he could not simply have Luther arrested and sent to Rome. It would seem to the princes (as well as to the peasant crowds) that Charles had betrayed traditional German liberties under pressure from an unpopular foreign power. And Frederick the Wise, whom Charles respected, and to whom he owed a debt of gratitude for supporting him in the imperial election, insisted that Luther be given a hearing, on German soil, before being consigned to the church. Charles reluctantly agreed that Luther could have a hearing at the imperial diet that was to meet at Worms in early 1521. He would be given a promise of safe conduct to travel to and from the diet, and would have to agree to refrain from publishing any more criticisms of the pope.

The church, naturally, was unhappy with Charles' decision, and pressured Charles to rescind his invitation to Luther and to prepare an imperial edict declaring Luther an outlaw. Such an edict would force Frederick and other sympathetic princes to cease their protection of Luther. Charles, apparently convinced that his religious duty was to do what was in his power to defeat Luther's heresy, agreed. But it would prove impossible for Charles to promulgate the edict. The public supported Luther, and the princes feared that refusing Luther his hearing would lead to revolts. Aleander, the papal ambassador, wrote that the clergy in Germany were nearly unanimous in their support of Luther.[31] "The whole of Germany," he wrote in his report, "is in full revolt; nine-tenths raise the war cry 'Luther,' while the watchword of the other tenth who are indifferent to Luther is 'Death to the Roman Curia.'"[32] Clearly, Luther would have to have at least a hearing. He set out from Wittenberg in March 1521, telling Staupitz, "This is not the time to be timid but to raise the voice loudly."[33]

So Luther arrived at Worms in April, three months after the diet had opened. He was enthusiastically greeted by crowds of supporters, and even received cordial visits from several of the princes. He hoped to give a public defense of his teaching, and was determined not to recant any portion of his teachings. He now saw the Roman church as a vital enemy—and he was determined to face it, even if it meant his death.

On April 17, at about 4:00 in the afternoon, he was led into the assembly hall where the princes were meeting. Charles was there, as were the political and ecclesiastical elites of Germany. On a table was a stack of Luther's books.

He was asked two questions: Had he written these books? If so, did he choose to recant any part of them? Luther, perhaps overawed by the pomp of the assembly, was uncharacteristically meek. He acknowledged that he had, in fact, written the books. As for the second question, he asked for some time to consider. He was granted a one-day respite. He returned to his room and seems to have recovered some degree of his bluster, for he wrote that evening to an acquaintance that "with Christ's help, however, I shall not in all eternity recant the least particle."[34]

The next day, he was not called before the diet until the evening. When he arrived, however, he was ready with his argument. The speech he gave echoes throughout history. He began by pointing out that he could not simply recant everything he had written—some were uncontroversial statements of Christian doctrine. He then went on to defend those works which attacked the papacy and church doctrine. He acknowledged that he had perhaps "been more bitter and vehement ... than is in keeping with my Christian estate and calling," but refused to recant anything because to do so would contribute to the papacy's tyranny over the spiritual lives of the people of God.[35]

The imperial spokesman cut Luther off and demanded that he give a clear, simple answer to the question. Luther concluded his speech at Worms with the following famous passage:

> Since your Imperial Majesty and Lordships demand a simple answer I will do so without horns or teeth as follows: Unless I am convicted by the testimony of Scripture or by evident reason (for I trust neither in popes nor councils alone, since it is obvious that they have often erred and contradicted themselves) I am convicted by the Scripture which I have mentioned and my conscience is captive to the Word of God. Therefore I cannot and will not recant, since it is difficult, unprofitable and dangerous indeed to do anything against one's conscience. God help me. Amen.[36]

The speech was published and quickly circulated throughout Germany. Luther's status as a folk hero was only improved by his defiant tone and his defense of individual conscience. But it did not end Luther's dealings at Worms.

Luther would not recant, but neither could Charles, who was after all a loyal Catholic, allow Luther to simply go free. But Charles was also a man of his word, and refused to violate the promise of safe conduct that he had extended to Luther. He would allow Luther 21 days to return to Wittenburg and to consider his position. He was instructed to refrain from preaching or writing. Once the safe conduct expired, however, Luther was to be officially condemned, and would be not only excommunicated, but an outlaw.

Chapter 4

CONFLICT AND REFORM

In the aftermath of the Diet of Worms, Luther had clearly broken with the church. He now had to face the vexing question of how to put his new theology into practice. Until 1521, Luther had worked primarily with abstract ideas. Now, he had firmly anchored himself to those ideas—primarily his commitment to justification by faith alone. But it remained to work out what those ideas actually meant for the average Christian. His defiance of the church had also unleashed forces that would ultimately prove impossible for him to fully control. He would find that many of his supporters would take his ideas further than he was comfortable with. The decade between 1521 and 1530 was, for Luther, a time of conflict over how to establish a truly reformed Christianity.

4.1 A Year of Exile

Luther and his companions set out from the Diet of Worms on April 26, having been ordered to return directly to Wittenberg. Before the party reached there, however, they were overtaken by a band of armed horsemen. These men grabbed Luther out of the wagon in which he was riding. They blindfolded him and dragged him off into the night. His companions did not know who had taken him or what would happen to him.

4.1.1 The Wartburg

Fortunately for Luther, the kidnapping had been the work of his patron, Frederick the Wise. Hoping to keep Luther safe from the imperial ban—and to prevent him from getting into any further trouble—he had arranged to have Luther kidnapped and hidden away until it was safe. Luther himself was apprised of the plan, but only in the most general terms, so he was legitimately surprised by the kidnapping. He was not happy about being taken into hiding, however. Frederick's plan had been kept remarkably secret from most everyone else. Most of Luther's friends and supporters assumed that he had been taken by forces loyal to the pope or the emperor, and that they would never see him again. Many assumed he had been killed. The painter Albrecht Durer, an admirer of Luther, wrote in his diary when he heard of Luther's disappearance:

> Oh God, if Luther is dead, who is going to proclaim the holy Gospel so clearly to us? Oh God, what could he have written in ten or twenty years? Oh, pious Christians, help me eagerly bewail this God-inspired man and pray that God may send us another.[1]

The location for his exile was to be the Wartburg, one of Frederick's castles. Located several miles from Eisenach, and largely vacant, the castle was far from prying eyes. Besides Luther, the only people there were the warden and two young servants. When he arrived, he was put up in a comfortable set of rooms, hidden behind a retractable staircase which could be closed up to hide Luther from any unexpected visitors. To further hide him from his enemies, he disguised himself as a knight, taking the name "Sir George." He let his monastic tonsure grow out, grew a knightly beard, and traded his monastic habits for the stylish garments of the landed gentry. He was comfortable, well-fed, and safe from his enemies. But he was far from happy about it.

When letters from the absent Luther began to make their way back to Wittenberg, his friends breathed a sigh of relief that he was safe. But Luther's letters reveal that he was unhappy about his situation. He was a man of action, and sitting around the Wartburg all day was not to his liking. He resented his absence from Wittenberg, where the reform movement was going on without him. He missed his friends, and he longed for something to do. His letters are full of language that depicts his time at the Wartburg as a kind of exile. The Wartburg was his "Patmos," referring to the island prison where the apostle John wrote the book of Revelation.[2]

The isolation also led to illness and depression. Luther was a social man, and being cooped up in a castle far from his friends and students took a strong toll on him. In early July, he wrote to his friend Philip Melanchthon that he was so bothered by a lesion that he was considering leaving the safety of the Wartburg to see a doctor.[3] He blamed most of his physical infirmities on the devil, who he believed was trying to end his ministry. Despite all of this, though, Luther accomplished a great deal during the ten months that he was in hiding.

4.1.2 The Bible in German

One way that Luther passed the time during his confinement was by writing. With little else to occupy him, he kept up an impressive pace at the Wartburg, churning out hundreds of pages worth of material. He wrote commentaries on several different biblical passages, pamphlets attacking his theological opponents, a lengthy treatise critiquing monastic vows, and a series of sermons to serve as models for his students. This flurry of writing also seems to have helped him work out, in his own mind, some of the practical implications of his theology. By far, though, the most significant piece of writing that emerged from Luther's time at the Wartburg was his translation of the New Testament into German.

Such a project was entirely consistent with his theological commitments. He was firmly committed to the supreme authority of the Bible over that of popes and church tradition. Furthermore, his assertion that all believers, and not just the clergy, had the right to interpret the Bible, expressed clearly in the *Address to the Christian Nobility*, made it imperative for average German Christians to have access to the Bible in their own language. Having little else to do, Luther placed tremendous energy into his translation, finishing the entire New Testament in an astonishing eleven weeks. Luther was not the first person to translate the scriptures into German, but his translation was unquestionably the most influential. Luther worked directly from the Greek text, unlike previous translators who had used the Latin Vulgate. His goal was to render the original text as closely as possible into the German language as it was actually spoken. He struggled to find the proper way to render the nuances of the original into German. For example, he wrote about his difficulty in finding an appropriate translation for Luke 1:28, in which the angel appears to Mary to announce the forthcoming birth of Jesus:

> Again, when the angel greets Mary, he says, "Hail Mary, full of grace, the Lord is with you." Up to now that has simply been translated according to the literal Latin. Tell me whether that is also good German? When does a German speak like that, "you are full of grace?" What German understands what that is, to be "full of grace?" He would have to think of a keg "full of" beer or a purse "full of" money. Therefore I have translated it, "Thou gracious one," so that a German can at least think his way through to what the angel meant by this greeting.[4]

Luther's method of translating produced a very accessible version of the New Testament, and one in which many of the subtleties of the Greek text came through clearly. His German New Testament was published in September

1522, and was an instant bestseller. The original print run of 3,000 copies quickly sold out and a second printing had to be done in December.

Luther was a fine scholar and his command of Greek was excellent, allowing him to undertake the translation of the New Testament on his own. The Old Testament was a slightly different story. Although Luther understood a great deal of Hebrew, he did not feel competent to translate the Old Testament on his own. His work at the Wartburg was thus limited to the 27 books of the New Testament. He was, however, determined to complete the project of translating the entire Bible. After his return from the Wartburg, he formed a committee of his fellow professors at Wittenberg to translate the Old Testament. This project went a good deal more slowly than had the New Testament, but a German version of the entire Bible, of which Luther was the chief translator, finally appeared in 1534.

Luther's German Bible was a landmark in German literature. Like the works of Shakespeare or the King James Bible in English, Luther's Bible helped to create the modern German language. The patterns and phrasings of Luther's Bible passed into the vernacular and became familiar to the German-speaking population of Europe. The clarity of Luther's translation was such that even his theological opponents made use of it. When the Catholic apologist Hieronymus Emser published his own version of the German Bible for the use of Catholics, he made extensive use of Luther's words and phrases.[5] German literary figures as diverse as Goethe, Frederick the Great, and Nietzsche have all praised Luther's Bible as the cornerstone of the German national identity. It also served as a model for other vernacular translations of the Bible, including William Tyndale's groundbreaking English translation.[6]

4.1.3 *Radicalization of the reform movement*

Papal and imperial forces may have chased Luther into hiding, but they could not stop his followers. While Luther was at the Wartburg, the reform movement continued to develop in Wittenberg. Despite his physical absence, Luther remained in touch with his colleagues by letter. He encouraged them to hold to the reformed teaching. He particularly encouraged his young protégée Philip Melanchthon—the Greek professor at Wittenberg—to take charge, and gave him specific instructions about how to respond to developments in the reform movement. Melanchthon was young and cautious, however, and was not able to provide the same kind of charismatic leadership that Luther had. So the primary leadership role in Wittenberg fell to Andreas Bodenstein von Karlstadt, the dean of the faculty at the university. Karlstadt was one of Luther's earliest converts, and had been the primary instigator of the Leipzig debate in 1519. Under his leadership, the Wittenberg reform movement became more radical. Luther had worked out a theology of justification by faith that cast much of Catholic practice into doubt, but had yet to reflect very deeply on how his ideas should be put into practice by the people. Karlstadt took the ideas that Luther had formulated and drew what he saw as the logical, practical conclusions. For instance, on Christmas Day 1521, he presided at a church service in street clothes, rather than the traditional clerical vestments. Contrary to traditional practice, he served both the bread and the wine of the Eucharist to the people. He began to preach vigorously against compulsory clerical celibacy and encouraged priests and monks to take wives. He demonstrated his commitment to clerical marriage when he was married to a 15-year-old girl on January 19, 1522. He attacked the use of images in worship and the practice of Gregorian chant. His sermons took on a fiery vigor, and he suggested that those who did not agree with his reforms were sinning against God. Another of Luther's Wittenberg colleagues, Gabriel Zwilling, began to destroy the statues, pictures, and crucifixes that he found in local chapels.

All of these reforms were drawn, to some degree, from Luther's ideas. Luther argued that the Bible alone should be the source of religious authority. Karlstadt could not find Biblical justification for the use of images, for clerical celibacy, or for special vestments—and so he threw them out. Luther's doctrine of the priesthood of all believers called into question any distinction between the clergy and the laity, and Karlstadt took that to mean that special dress or privileges for the clergy were unacceptable. The suddenness and aggressiveness of his changes took the people by surprise though, and many were deeply wounded by his assertion that their traditional religious practices were actually sinful.

As Karlstadt was instituting these changes, reform-minded people from throughout Saxony were finding their way to Wittenberg. In particular, a group of three young men from the nearby town of Zwickau arrived in Wittenberg shortly after Christmas 1521. These so-called "Zwickau prophets"—two weavers and a former theology student of Luther's—claimed to have had direct, mystical revelations from God. They began to teach that the bread and wine of the Eucharist were only symbolic and did not actually contain Jesus' real presence. They preached against infant baptism, since in the New Testament baptism is always accompanied by a confession of faith, which was not possible for very small children to make.

Karlstadt was impressed with the Zwickau prophets and their theology, but Melanchthon was uncertain about them and wrote nervously to Luther for instruction. Luther insisted that Melanchthon treat claims of special revelation with skepticism and reasserted that it was only the Bible, and not private revelations, that revealed God's plan for human salvation.[7] He was also alarmed by the Zwickau prophets' assault on the real effectiveness of the sacraments as an attack on the very heart of Christianity. To be sure, Luther had criticized the Catholic doctrine of transubstantiation, but he had never—and never would—reject the idea that Christ was truly present in the sacraments, and that the sacraments, when accompanied by true faith, had real effect.

Before long, the more radical teachings of Karlstadt and the Zwickau prophets came to fruition among the townspeople. On December 3, a group of armed students and townspeople forcefully stopped a monk from reading a private mass in the town church. In January, a group of rioters broke into the town church, destroying furniture, statues, and paintings. Elector Frederick was furious at these disturbances of the peace, and called for Luther's return from the Wartburg, hoping the charismatic reformer's presence would serve to calm the frenzied atmosphere in Wittenberg.

4.1.4 *Return from exile*

Luther returned to Wittenberg in early March 1522. He was still technically an outlaw, and the Emperor might choose to enforce the edict that had outlawed him at the Diet of Worms. This might compel Frederick to turn Luther over to an imperial court. Nevertheless, Luther began to preach openly in Wittenberg on March 9. Distancing himself from Karlstadt's dramatic reforms, he appeared dressed in traditional monastic robes. He preached a series of eight sermons in which he called for restraint and order. Violence and coercion, he argued, had no place in the true Christian life. Changes in practice should be introduced gradually, and only after careful reflection. Some people were not yet ready to embrace the sorts of reforms that Karlstadt was suggesting, and those who were ready must be patient with those who were not. Luther preached that

> one must not insist upon his rights, but must see what may be helpful to his brother, as Paul says, "all things are lawful for me, but not all things are helpful." For we are not all equally strong in faith, some of you have a stronger faith than I. Therefore we must not look upon ourselves, or our strength, or our prestige, but upon our neighbor, for God has said through Moses: I have borne and reared you, as a mother does her child. What does a mother do to her child? First she gives it milk, then gruel, then eggs and soft food, whereas if she turned about and gave it solid food, the child would never thrive. So we should also deal with our brother, have patience with him for a time, have patience with his weakness and help him bear it, we should give him milk-food too, as

was done with us, until he, too, grows strong, and thus we do not travel heavenward alone, but bring our brethren, who are not now our friends, with us [...] The cause is good, but there has been too much haste. For there are still brothers and sisters on the other side who belong to us and must still be won.[8]

Luther was clearly concerned that the pace of reform would alienate those who were not yet ready for dramatic changes in practice, but he also worried that forcing changes upon the people from the top down was in direct opposition to his doctrine of justification by faith alone. It was not the externals of the faith—things like church practices—that reconciled the sinner to God, but rather faith alone that saved. If the Wittenberg reformers were to get too caught up in changing church practices, it might seem that those practices, rather than faith in the promise of Christ, were marks of a true Christian. In a later sermon, talking about Karlstadt's introduction of serving both the bread and the wine of the Eucharist, Luther forcibly made the point that external practices do not make one holy: "If you desire to be regarded as better Christians than others just because you take the sacrament into your own hands and receive it in both kinds, you are bad Christians as far as I am concerned."[9]

These sermons had an immediate calming effect. Order was restored. The Zwickau prophets were ushered out of town, and Karlstadt, whose relationship with Luther was deeply damaged, soon left Wittenberg as well. The more radical innovations that had been introduced during Luther's absence were mostly rescinded, and calm gradually returned. One student summed up the impact of Luther's sermons thus: "All week long Luther did nothing other than to put back in place what we had knocked down, and he took us all severely to task."[10]

But these disturbances are one of the earliest indications that the forces that Luther had set in motion would be impossible for him to fully control. Luther forcefully asserted that the Bible should be the sole source of religious authority. But, in the absence of an authoritative church to determine what the Bible *means*, different people may understand the Bible's teachings differently. This seems to be what happened with Karlstadt. His attempts at reform all seem to have been drawn from his reading of the Bible. But he clearly understood the implications of the Biblical text differently than did Luther.

The disturbances in Wittenberg during his absence also illustrate something of Luther's theological conservatism. While Luther often appears to be a radical, in reality he sought to retain as much as he could of the traditions and practices of the church. He defended infant baptism and the real presence of

Christ in the bread and wine of the Eucharist. In conscious opposition to the radicals, he supported the use of art in the churches as well.

Luther had reclaimed leadership of the reform movement in Wittenberg and restored order. The violence and upheavals that had marked the period of Luther's absence ended, and the city grew calm again. But it would not remain so forever, and Luther was soon faced with another, more violent upheaval.

4.2 The Peasants' War

In 1524, political revolts started to spread among the German peasants. In itself, this was nothing new. There had been similar uprisings in Germany for hundreds of years. The peasants were often unhappy about high taxation, failing harvests, and the sense that landlords were not treating the peasants with appropriate justice. What was new in 1524 was the way in which the peasants incorporated Luther's theological positions into their revolt. If, as Luther taught, all Christians were free from the oppressive hierarchy of the church and able to read the Bible for themselves, it seemed to follow that they should also be free from the oppressive hierarchy of their landlords and be able to order their political affairs according to their own understanding.

The peasants' grievances were outlined in February 1525, in a series of articles written by a tanner and lay reformer, Sebastian Lotzer, and a Lutheran pastor, Christoph Schappeler. The *Twelve Articles*, as they came to be known, call for a series of mostly political reforms. Most of these were fairly typical for peasant uprisings. They claimed, for instance, that the peasants should be able to hunt, fish, and gather firewood without persecution. Taxes should be lowered and made fairer. But the *Twelve Articles* went further than previous peasant uprisings, and seem to have been directly influenced by Luther's theology. Each of the demands in the *Twelve Articles* is supported by references to the Bible, and the entire document was concluded with a pledge to retract any demand that could be shown to be contrary to the Bible.[11]

By mixing together Lutheran theology and the traditional concerns of the peasants against their landlords, the *Twelve Articles* set the stage for an enormous rebellion of Germany's peasants. Luther's Catholic opponents were aghast. They argued that the social dislocation threatened by the *Twelve Articles* was the direct and natural outgrowth of Luther's rejection of papal authority. The peasants, believing that their demands were sanctioned by God, were inflexible and refused to compromise. The landlords were equally stubborn. The situation was made more dramatic by the fact that many of the German landlords were wealthy monasteries and abbeys. Thus, in many cases, the political rebellion of the peasants was also, in a very real sense, a revolt against the church. This made Luther's criticism of the church a powerful weapon in the hands of the peasant leaders.

Luther himself received a copy of the *Twelve Articles* in April 1525 and replied with a short treatise called *An Admonition to Peace*. In it, Luther sympathized with the peasants' concerns and reproached the princes and landlords:

> We have no one on earth to thank for this disastrous rebellion, except you princes and lords, especially you blind bishops and mad priests and monks, whose hearts are hardened, even to the present day [...] you do nothing but cheat and rob the people so that you may lead a life of luxury and extravagance. The poor common people cannot bear it any longer. The sword is already at your throats, but you think that you sit so firm in the saddle that no one can unhorse you. This false security and stubborn perversity will break your necks, as you will discover.[12]

Turning to the peasants, Luther condemned the use of violence against the social order that God had set in place. The princes were in the wrong, he wrote, but armed rebellion against them was equally wrong. "Christians," he claimed, "do not fight for themselves with sword and musket, but with the cross and with suffering, just as Christ, our leader, does not bear a sword, but hangs on the cross."[13] He advised both sides to settle the dispute peacefully, because if they persisted in their stubbornness, they might bring about the destruction of all Germany.

But the revolt had spread too far to be quelled by peaceful negotiations. Massive rebellion spread throughout Germany. Luther saw the destruction caused by the revolt first-hand while travelling in Thuringia, where he was threatened and heckled by groups of violent peasants. He also began to receive reports of atrocities committed by groups of rebellious peasants, and of cities forced to surrender to the rebels. It became clear to him that his call for a peaceful resolution of the revolt had fallen on deaf ears. He began to worry that the peasants' revolt would lead to massive political disorder and chaos. He may have felt some responsibility for the revolt, given that his theology had encouraged the peasants. So, in May, he wrote the vicious *Against the Robbing and Murdering Hordes of Peasants*, a tract which surprised many of his friends and allies with its aggressive tone.

Unlike his earlier *Admonition to Peace*, this treatise was angry and violent. In it Luther forcefully called upon the princes to put down the peasants' revolt by any means necessary. Rebellion, he claimed, was a kind of disease which, if not stopped, will eventually overrun all of society:

> For rebellion is not just simple murder, it is like a great fire, which attacks and devastates a whole land. Thus rebellion brings with it a land filled with murder and bloodshed; it makes widows and orphans, and turns everything upside down, like the worst disaster. Therefore let everyone who can, smite, slay, and stab, secretly or openly, remembering that nothing can be more poisonous than a rebel. It is just as when one must kill a mad dog; if you do not strike him, he will strike you, and the whole land with you.[14]

This sort of rhetoric quite understandably alienated many of Luther's supporters. The mayor of Zwickau wrote to an associate in June 1525 that Luther's reaction to the uprising was rash and that Luther had almost completely lost the support of the peasants.[15] Consequently he tried to explain his position in a third tract, *An Open Letter on the Harsh Book Against the Peasants*, printed in July 1525.[16] In it, he explained that his harshness had been directed against those peasants who were obdurate and who refused to listen to reason. God, he argued, had given the princes the duty to restrain evil and to promote social order. It was, therefore, their Christian calling to put down rebellions. If the people would not listen to reason, the princes must resort to the use of force.

Luther's reaction to the Peasants' War is very similar to his reaction to Karlstadt and the radical reformers of 1521–22. In both cases, Luther urged that social order was vital, and that dramatic change of any sort was to be resisted. For Luther, as for nearly everybody else in the sixteenth century, governments had been instituted by God, and were used by God for his purposes. Even governments that opposed true religion were divinely ordained. Because of this, Luther rejected any attempt to overthrow the existing social order. On the other hand, despite his enthusiastic support of the princes' right to use violence against rebels, he remained steadfast in his belief that violence should not be used to support or enforce the gospel.

But Luther could not afford to linger over his response to the peasants' revolt. There was to be much more for Luther to address in 1525. At the same time, he was calling on the princes to put down the rebellion, he was also engaged in fierce debates with two men who ought to have been his allies: the Swiss reformer Ulrich Zwingli and the Dutch humanist Desiderius Erasmus.

4.3 Zwingli and the Conflict over the Eucharist

Luther's followers in Wittenberg were not the only ones calling for reform of the church in the 1520s. Dozens of church leaders throughout Germany followed Luther's example and broke from the Catholic Church. One of the earliest, Martin Bucer, was present at the Heidelberg Disputation and had been so impressed with Luther that he began to institute Lutheran-style reforms in his native Strasbourg. Numerous others followed. Many took Luther's theology as their starting point, but differed from Luther in their theological details.

There was also a reform movement, similar to Luther's, brewing south of Germany in Switzerland. The Swiss reformers seem to have arrived at much the same conclusions as had Luther—but they seem to have done so more-or-less independently of Luther. The leader of this movement was Ulrich Zwingli, a priest from Zurich. Shortly after the 95 Theses, Zwingli began to preach a message of reform in Zurich that included many of the same themes as Luther had proposed in Wittenberg. Like Luther, Zwingli saw the Bible as the ultimate authority for Christian teaching and taught that salvation came through faith rather than through the sacraments.

Zwingli's teachings were a good deal more far-reaching than Luther's, though. Whereas Luther clearly wanted to proceed carefully and to retain as much of the Catholic tradition as was compatible with his reformed understanding of the gospel, Zwingli's goal was to aggressively root out anything for which there was no explicit Biblical justification. Thus, while Luther was comfortable with retaining many traditional practices such as the observance of Lent, Zwingli, who could find no mention of Lent in the Bible, rejected the Lenten fast. This marks a key difference in approach between the two men, which will ultimately come to characterize the churches that develop from their teachings. Luther, and later Lutheran churches, retained as much as they could of the old Church, only eliminating practices that were clearly contrary to the gospel. Zwingli, and later Reformed churches, had a tendency to eliminate everything that was associated with the old church, and to build a new church from the ground up, based wholly upon reformed principles.

By far the most significant difference between Luther and Zwingli was in their respective understanding of the sacraments, and particularly of the Eucharist. Although he rejected much Catholic teaching about the nature of the Eucharist, Luther was a firm defender of Jesus' real presence in the bread and the wine. Zwingli taught that the bread and wine were only symbols of Christ's body and blood. For Zwingli, the real purpose of the Eucharist was to memorialize Christ's death and resurrection—not to convey Jesus' physical presence to the worshiper. His position was very similar to that taught by the Zwickau Prophets and adopted by Karlstadt during Luther's exile at the Wartburg, and Luther seems to have associated a symbolic understanding of the Eucharist with the political unrest that accompanied Karlstadt's reforms of 1521–1522. So he proved to be singularly unwilling to compromise with Zwingli over the proper understanding of the Eucharist.

Between 1525 and 1529, Luther and Zwingli, along with their respective supporters, published pamphlet after pamphlet attacking one another's views of the Eucharist. Luther and Zwingli were both stubborn men and both firmly believed that the Bible supported their position, so the exchanges between the two men grew increasingly bitter and personal. Here again is an example of the key problem that Luther would continue to face during the 1520s and 1530s. In the absence of a church hierarchy to authoritatively interpret the Bible, individual believers tend to come to different conclusions about what the Bible actually means. So resolving theological disputes solely on the basis of the Bible alone proved to be difficult, if not impossible.

Other reformers of more pacific temperaments tried to work out a compromise between the two men, but without success. The rift between the two reformers threatened to overturn the successes of both, as both turned their energies to attacking one another. Many who were sympathetic to reform thought that Luther and Zwingli ought to set aside their doctrinal differences so that the reformers could present a united front to the Emperor and the Catholics. If they insisted on directing their energy into quarrels between themselves, they could never hope to stand up to the more powerful forces of the Church and the Empire.

It was Philip of Hesse, a leading German prince and supporter of Luther, who made the greatest effort to reconcile Luther and Zwingli. Philip saw the dispute between the reformers as a military liability. He was trying to build an alliance of reform-minded princes to oppose the Imperial army, and he couldn't afford to lose potential allies over what he saw as an insignificant piece of theological hairsplitting. He managed to arrange a meeting between Luther and Zwingli at his capital city of Marburg in 1529. At the Marburg Colloquy, as the meeting came to be known, the two reformers agreed to a somewhat ambiguous statement of faith, but could not come to common agreement on the question of the real presence in the Eucharist. Luther insisted that the words 'this is my body,' spoken by Jesus in the Gospel of Luke must be taken literally; Zwingli was just as insistent that they were intended figuratively or symbolically. The two men left the Colloquy dissatisfied, and their followers diverged into two theologically similar, but distinct, reforming churches. Luther's followers, soon known as "Lutherans," became prominent in northern Germany and spread into Scandinavia. The followers of Zwingli, who would ultimately include John Calvin, the great reformer of Geneva, would loosely become known as "reformed" churches. These two traditions, although they shared many basic doctrinal commitments, developed distinctive theologies, institutions, and practices. And although they occasionally worked together, the two groups never fully reconciled with one another.

The controversy over the Eucharist illustrates a problem that would loom large in Protestant theology. Both Luther and Zwingli appealed to the Bible alone as their source of authority, yet they came to dramatically different conclusions about what the Bible actually *meant*. Without the authority of an institutional church to determine the correct interpretation of the Bible, there is no way to judge between two different readings of the Bible. So the Protestant movement would ultimately be prone to fracture every time a doctrinal controversy arose, for without an authoritative way to determine how the Bible should be understood, each side of the dispute held doggedly to their own Biblical understandings.

4.4 Erasmus and the Bondage of the Will

A different sort of conflict arose between Luther and the eminent Dutch humanist Desiderius Erasmus. Luther initially admired Erasmus, who also called for a reform of corruption within the church. Erasmus, like Luther, urged Christians to return to the scriptures, and prepared the critical Greek edition of the New Testament that Luther used to translate it into German. Even after Luther's excommunication, Erasmus refused to publicly denounce Luther. Many people across Europe associated Luther with Erasmus, and there were even widespread rumors that the works circulating under Luther's name had actually been written by Erasmus![17] Even though Erasmus remained loyal to the Catholic Church, Luther and his friends must have held out hope that the great humanist would support them, or at least refuse to oppose them. Luther even wrote an extremely friendly letter to Erasmus in 1519, indicating his respect for the great humanist, and clearly holding out hope that he and Erasmus could work together for common cause.[18]

But Erasmus and Luther were more fundamentally different than they appeared to be. Although they were both critics of the church, they came to their criticism from dramatically different places. Erasmus' basic message was that the church was worldly, corrupt, and hostile to learning. For Erasmus, true Christianity lay in loving God and ones' neighbors. The solution to the problems facing the church was simply to remove the corruptions that had crept in. Luther's concerns, on the other hand, were essentially about the church's doctrine. For Luther, the corruption and worldliness in the church were symptoms of a deeper problem—the fact that the church encouraged people to try to earn their salvation through the sacraments and good works.

That there was a deep disagreement between the two men was not a new development in 1525. Even before the *95 Theses*, Luther had written several letters in which, although he admired Erasmus' willingness to criticize corruption within the church, he expressed discomfort with some of the implications of Erasmus' theology.[19] The root of Luther's discomfort lay in Erasmus' apparent assumption that moral behavior—following the Biblical laws—was necessary in order to be saved. Erasmus, too, recognized that he and Luther were not on exactly the same page theologically. He wrote to a friend in 1522 in frustration that both the Lutherans and the Papacy thought that he (Erasmus) was working for the other side.[20]

Perhaps in order to demonstrate to his Catholic friends that he was not actually a Lutheran, in 1524 Erasmus wrote a tract, *On the Freedom of the Will*, which directly attacked Luther's theology.[21] Erasmus begins with the suggestion that some doctrines, like free will, are mysterious and not possible for humans to fully understand.[22] More substantially, Erasmus argued that a person's good deeds could, at least in some small way, contribute to his or her salvation. This must be so, claims Erasmus for two reasons. First, if people's good works did not have some real effect, then there would be no reason for people to behave morally. To teach, as Luther did, that salvation is entirely in the hands of God and that the sinner can do nothing to affect his or her salvation would encourage all manner of public misbehavior. Furthermore, Erasmus claimed, if humans do not have free will, it would make God morally reprehensible, since he punishes sinners for something that they have no ability to overcome. He sums up his position like this:

> Suppose for a moment that it were true in a certain sense, as Augustine says somewhere, that "God works in us good and evil, and rewards his own good works in us, and punishes his evil works in us;" what a window to impiety would be the public avowal of such an opinion open to countless mortals! Especially in view of the slowness of mind of mortal men, their sloth, their malice, and their incurable propensity toward all manner of evil. What weakling will be able to bear the endless and wearisome warfare against his flesh? What evildoer will take pains to correct his life? Who will be able to bring himself to love God with all his heart when He created hell seething with eternal torments in order to punish his own misdeeds in his victims as though he took delight in human torments?[23]

It's a strong argument, and one that effectively points out some practical drawbacks to Luther's position. But Erasmus doesn't deny that human free will is extremely limited. He likens the human will to a small child who wants to pick an apple. When the child cannot reach the apple, his father lifts him up and helps him to pick the apple. In no way did the child pick the apple on his own, but the child did not depend entirely on the father either. In the same way, for Erasmus, individual humans cooperate with God to achieve the goal of salvation.[24]

Luther responded instantly, and with vigor. "It is unbelievable," he wrote to a friend, "how much the book on the freedom of the will nauseates me."[25] Luther's disdain reflects the fact that Erasmus had identified a central issue in his theology, and had made an effective argument against it. Luther's reply, *The Bondage of the Will*, is three times as long as Erasmus' work.[26] Luther begins by praising Erasmus for identifying a central issue and for not wasting time on trivialities. He then goes on to give an extensive response to Erasmus' arguments. Luther found this book so effective that, when he was asked at the end of his life which of his hundreds of works were the most valuable, he replied that only his catechisms and *The Bondage of the Will* were of lasting importance.[27]

Luther first takes issue with Erasmus' assertion that the freedom or bondage of the will was an issue that Christians could not fully understand. For Luther, it was vital that Christians be able to trust God's promises with certainty:

> Now, since God has taken my salvation out of my hands into his, making it depend on his choice and not mine, and has promised to save me, not by my own work or exertion but by his grace and mercy, I am assured and certain both that he is faithful and will not lie to me, and also that he is too great and powerful for any demons or any adversaries to be able to break him or to snatch me from him.[28]

He goes on to reaffirm his central insight that saving people from their sins is an action that belongs entirely to God, and that human efforts—however well-intentioned—can never achieve salvation. The human will, for Luther, is too weak. He compares it to a donkey which must be led by its owners. If the will is not controlled by God, Luther reasons, it will be under the control of Satan.[29] Luther bases his assessment not only on his personal experience, but on his literal reading of the Bible. While Erasmus was horrified to think that God might not be good in the sense that the Renaissance humanists defined goodness, Luther was concerned only to be faithful to the way that God reveals himself in the scriptures. Roland Bainton pithily summed the dispute up as Erasmus saying that God must be *good*, and Luther replying that we must let God be *God*.[30]

For Luther, then the only course of action available to human beings is to trust in God's work rather than our own efforts:

> For if we believe it to be true that God foreknows and predestines all things, that he can neither be mistaken in his foreknowledge nor hindered in his predestination, and that nothing takes place but as he wills it (as reason itself is forced to admit), then on the testimony of reason itself there cannot be any free choice in man or angel or any creature. Similarly, if we believe that Satan is the ruler of this world, who is forever plotting and fighting against the Kingdom of Christ with all his powers, and that he will not let men go who are his captives unless he is forced to do so by the divine power of the Spirit, then again it is evident that there can be no such thing as free choice… To sum up: If we believe that Christ has redeemed men by his blood, we are bound to confess that the whole man was lost; otherwise, we should make Christ either superfluous or the redeemer of only the lowest part of man, which would be blasphemy and sacrilege.[31]

Luther's book is overwhelming in the volume of scripture he uses to support his position that a faithful reading of the Bible insists upon the human will's complete submission to God. *The Bondage of the Will* is one of Luther's most difficult books, but also one of the most central to understanding his thought. Modern readers may find it hard to admire Luther's insistence on our own inability to do anything for ourselves, but Luther would have identified the modern obsession with our own abilities as a symptom of our society's spiritual illness. All told, *The Bondage of the Will* is a compelling expression of two of the most important themes in Luther's theology: justification by faith alone and the absolute authority of the scriptures.

4.5 The Augsburg Confession

As Luther was busy exploring the implications of his new theology and defining its limits, support for him was growing in Germany. Luther was fortunate to have the political support of his own prince, and as his teachings spread throughout Europe, more and more political leaders allied themselves with Luther's camp. Frederick the Wise, whose personal religious adherence was carefully enigmatic, doggedly supported Luther and protected him from both the Pope and the Emperor. He allowed Luther and his followers to preach in Electoral Saxony and took action to prevent Luther's capture and to keep him from harm. He did not, however, break with Rome or seek to establish a separate church. Many of the imperial towns, however, did rush to Luther's side despite the opposition of both Pope and Emperor. These cities, which enjoyed relative independence from both the princes and the Emperor, became important centers of reformation thought and practice.[32]

After his excommunication at the Diet of Worms, Luther was placed under an imperial ban. This meant, at least in theory, that the princes were bound to oppose Luther and to turn him over to Imperial authorities for punishment. Despite this, several princes were sympathetic to Luther and did little or nothing to actually enforce the ban. The princes likely recognized Luther's popularity with the people, and feared that taking a public stand against Luther would result in popular uprisings. They may also have seen in Luther's split with the church an opportunity to increase their own power. And some seem to have been genuinely converted to Luther's theological positions.

As time ran on, a split emerged among the princes. Some became bitter opponents of Luther, blaming him for disrupting the social fabric by defying both church and Emperor. Among these was George, the leader of Ducal Saxony and Frederick the Wise's cousin. George would emerge as one of Luther's most vocal critics during the early 1520s. The Peasants' War forced many of these princes to take a firmer stand against Luther. They saw him as a clear threat to the public order and feared that, if he were not stopped, more violence would follow in his wake.

Other princes supported Luther. Frederick the Wise, although not openly Lutheran, was certainly Luther's chief protector. And when Frederick died in 1525, his successor, John the Steadfast, became an open supporter of the Protestants and took action to impose Lutheran reforms in his territory.

Meanwhile, the emperor's attention continued to be distracted. Even though he steadfastly opposed Luther, Charles had other important matters clamoring for his attention. He was worried about the growing threat to central Europe posed by the Turks, who would successfully attack Hungary in 1526. He was at war with the French, quarrelling with the Pope, who was supporting his French enemy, and struggling to maintain order in all corners of his diverse empire. The last thing Charles needed in the 1520s was a religious power struggle in Germany. So, in an attempt to resolve the issues raised by Luther, Charles asked the Imperial Diet, to be held in Speyer in 1526, to resolve the Luther question.

Although Charles himself did not attend the Diet of Speyer, he sent his brother, Archduke Ferdinand of Austria to represent him. The assembled princes, recognizing that they would not be able to resolve the religious issues to everyone's satisfaction, decided to defer judgment on Luther and his reforms to a church council to be held in the near future. Until a council could make an authoritative decision about Luther, the princes vowed to "conduct their affairs as they hope and trust to answer to God and his imperial majesty."[33] The ambiguity of this formulation allowed the individual princes to decide for themselves the extent to which they would enforce Luther's imperial ban. Several reform-minded princes used the formulation adopted at Speyer to begin to implement reforms in their territory.

Another Imperial Diet met in Speyer four years later. At this second Diet of Speyer, the princes opposed to reform tried to rescind the 1526 edict and reestablish strict enforcement of Luther's ban. By this time, however, enough support for Luther had developed among the princes that a substantial group of reform-minded princes issued a formal protest against such heavy-handed treatment of Luther and his supporters. These princes were labeled "Protestants," and the name became firmly associated with Luther's religious reform movement. The presence of a substantial group of reforming princes at the 1529 Diet of Speyer also convinced Charles and his advisors that they needed to act quickly to resolve the religious question once and for all. Charles, who had not been at either of the Speyer diets, returned to Germany for the first time in almost ten years in order to personally attend the next Imperial Diet, set to meet in Augsburg in 1530. It was at Augsburg, Charles hoped, that the Luther question would be settled once and for all.

When he received his summons to attend the Diet at Augsburg, the new Saxon Elector, John the Steadfast, called Luther, along with three of his close associates, to his court at Torgau. John asked the theologians to write a summary of their faith to be presented to the Emperor at the Diet. Although the primary author was the more mild-mannered Philip Melanchthon, the ideas represented were all Luther's. After seeing Melanchthon's draft, Luther responded, "I know nothing to improve or change it, nor would this be appropriate, since I cannot step so softly and quietly."[34] This document, the *Augsburg Confession*, would become a definitive statement of the Lutheran faith. Melanchthon, who still hoped that the Protestant movement might reconcile with Rome, strove to emphasize the doctrinal agreements between the Lutheran party and the Catholics. Thus he opened the *Augsburg Confession* with 22 articles that outline the common Christian faith that the Lutherans and the Catholics shared. The final seven articles describe doctrinal disagreements. The Lutherans insisted on offering both the bread and the wine during the Eucharist—against traditional Catholic practice. They also allowed priests to marry, and denied that the Mass, confession of sins to a priest, fasting, and monastic vows possessed any power to save souls. Finally, the Lutherans rejected the secular authority of bishops.[35]

The *Augsburg Confession* is a carefully constructed and, considering the circumstances, a remarkably conciliatory document. Its authors hoped the confession would help to reconcile them with the Catholic Church. It is, in fact, far less provocative than much of Luther's rhetoric. Some twenty-first-century Catholic scholars—including Pope Benedict XVI—have suggested that the *Augsburg Confession* could be construed as a faithfully Catholic statement of faith, and believe that ecumenical discussions between Lutherans and Catholics could use this document as a foundation.[36]

The confession was signed by Elector John and six other Lutheran princes, as well as the mayors and city councils of two imperial cities: Nuremberg and Reutlingen. John and most of his retinue left for Augsburg, but Luther stayed behind in Coburg. He was still an outlaw and couldn't risk travelling through territory controlled by Catholic princes. He stayed in close touch by letter with Melanchthon, who would be the chief negotiator for the Lutherans.

The Lutheran princes had the *Augsburg Confession* read in its entirety at the Diet—a task that took more than two hours! Emperor Charles listened politely, and then appointed a committee of theologians to examine and refute it. A week after the Lutherans had read their confession a Catholic response was similarly read aloud at the Diet. In Charles' estimation the Lutherans had been effectively refuted, and he ordered Melanchthon and the princes to recant. When they refused to do so, Charles intended to go to war against them to force their submission.

He softened his position, however, when the Catholic princes who were in attendance at Augsburg refused to endorse a war. They were not particularly concerned about the maintenance of doctrinal purity, but were quite worried about the potential growth of imperial power that might result from such a civil war. Charles was backed into a corner. He couldn't go to war, and he refused to appeal to a church council to resolve the issue.[37] This meant that he couldn't, at this time, do anything about the defection of the Lutheran princes. The Diet of Augsburg can thus be seen as the beginning of a new era for Luther and his followers. They had stood up to the Emperor, and the Emperor had blinked.

Chapter 5

A NEW WAY TO BE A CHRISTIAN

Between 1522 and 1530, Luther and his colleagues began to develop a new expression of Christianity, which they called *Evangelical*. The word comes from the Greek term for gospel, and reflects that Luther and his followers saw themselves as particularly focused on the gospel of Christ. The movement would, much later, become known as Lutheran. The Evangelicals had broken decisively with the Catholic Church over doctrine and were now developing their own distinctive institutions and practices. But they were convinced that they remained Christians—more truly Christian, in fact, than the Pope and the Catholic hierarchy.

5.1 Basic Themes in Luther's Theology

Because of the large number and diverse nature of Luther's written works, it is sometimes difficult to construct a general statement about the nature of Luther's theology. Certainly, however, there are several key themes which recur throughout his writings and it is worthwhile to pause for a moment to describe some of these main themes.

5.1.1 *Justification by faith alone*

When Luther looked back on his career at the end of his life, he identified the discovery of justification by faith as the decisive turning point in his career.[1] Luther's conviction that humans were reconciled to God entirely through faith in Christ—rather than through their own efforts or their religious acts—is the central idea of the Reformation. "I teach," Luther said, "that people should trust in nothing but Jesus Christ alone, not in prayers or merits or even in their own works."[2]

Luther starts with the observation that humans are incapable of living the kind of perfectly sinless life that the Bible seems to mandate. This is what gave him such a troubled conscience as a young man. He recognized that he couldn't live up to the high standards of righteousness that were outlined in the scriptures. The church had addressed this concern by instituting the sacrament of penance, by which people could atone for their sins. Even so, Luther saw little hope of anybody achieving the state of true repentance necessary for the sacrament to be effective. In practice, many believers, and Luther chief among them, participated in the sacrament of penance not because they actually repented of their sins, but rather because they feared divine punishment. In this case, Luther reasoned, the sacrament is done for a purely selfish motive. Thus, it seemed to Luther perfectly hopeless to expect that sinful human beings could ever be reconciled to God under the sacramental system.

His solution for this difficulty is strikingly simple. We are saved, says Luther, not by the things we do, but by faith alone. By faith he doesn't mean the intellectual assent to doctrines, but rather a wholehearted trust in the promise of God. So Luther came to see justification—being made right with God—as something that is done for us, rather than something that we do. In 1518, Luther outlined this position in his *Explanations of the 95 Theses*:

> People must be taught that if they really want to find peace for their consciences they should learn to place their confidence, not in the power of the pope, but in the word of Christ who gives the promise to the pope. For it is not because the pope grants it that you have anything, but you have it because you believe that you receive it. You have only as much as you believe according to the promise of Christ.[3]

The key here is that Luther sees God as the only actor. We cannot save ourselves. But God can act to save us. And he does. So Luther—a man who had no confidence in his own efforts at righteousness—shifted his confidence from himself to God. God's promise, found in the scriptures and embodied in the sacraments, was all that Luther needed.

The flip side of this was that any teaching that suggested that people could or ought to do something to merit their own salvation was, for Luther, deeply mistaken. He found this kind of thinking to be not only against the clear teachings of scripture, but also deeply dangerous to the individual soul. If people think that they deserve salvation because of their good works, it will lead to arrogance and smug self-satisfaction. If, on the other hand, people become convinced that they need to do something to merit God's grace—as Luther had been convinced as a young man—they can become trapped in their own anxieties. They will be always wondering whether they have done enough, or whether their good works were done for the right reasons. Instead, Luther insisted, sinners should simply trust in God's promise to save them in spite of themselves.

This explains why Luther was so troubled by Tetzel's indulgence peddling in 1517. If human actions like buying indulgences could merit God's grace, then those sinners who bought indulgences would be trusting in their purchases rather than in God's promises. Furthermore, those who were not able to buy indulgences might be cast into despair by their inability to take advantage of this opportunity to make peace with God. In any case, the sale of indulgences clearly implied that you needed to take some action in order to earn the forgiveness of your sins. The same was true for Luther's dispute with Erasmus over the freedom of the will. Luther saw in Erasmus' theology the idea that people could do something to merit salvation.

Out of this key idea developed Luther's distinctive idea that Christians are *simul justus et peccator*—at the same time both righteous and sinful.[4] The formulation reflects Luther's love of paradoxical phrases, but also promotes the idea that human beings are made right with God through divine fiat rather than through actually purging their souls of sin. The sinner is righteous in the eyes of God because he accepts the promise of Christ. He also remains sinful in and of himself as a human being.[5]

Justification by faith alone became, for Luther and his followers, the "article upon which the church stands or falls." This single doctrine colored the rest of Luther's theological world. It remains a key teaching for Protestants to this very day.

5.1.2 *The authority of scripture*

The second key element in Luther's theology is his insistence that the only authoritative source for Christian doctrine was the Bible. This doctrine has become known in Protestant circles as *sola scriptura*. Luther seems to have become convinced relatively early in his career that sinners were justified by faith alone. When he began to teach this new doctrine, and particularly when he became involved in the crises that arose following the publication of the 95 *Theses*, he found that the church hierarchy and the byzantine maze of scholastic theology seemed to stand in the way of his reformation discovery.

Thus, Luther came to distrust the church authorities and scholastic theology as arbiters of doctrine. The idea that the Bible itself, rather than church doctrine or papal pronouncements, was the only source of Christian doctrine gave Luther some important leverage in his arguments against the papacy. This was an effective way to support his position, but it was risky.

Luther's opponents between 1517 and 1520 tended to accuse him on just this point. The Bible is a complicated book and needed to be not just read but interpreted. How could one solitary monk, they argued, challenge the teachings of the entire church?

Luther had little patience with this sort of argument. It seemed to him to miss the main point. Instead of engaging what Luther felt was the vital issue of how sinners could be reconciled to God, his opponents such as Cajetan and Eck wanted to hide behind the authority of the church. Over the course of his disputes with them, Luther became convinced that popes and councils could err, and came to believe firmly that the scripture alone was authoritative. Thus, at Worms in 1521, he justified his refusal to recant by claiming the exclusive authority of scripture and demanding that he be shown the error of his ways not through papal pronouncements, but through the scriptures.

The doctrine of *sola scriptura* implied a dramatic reevaluation of the value of scholastic theology. Luther rejected the Aristotelian methods of medieval theology, and suspected medieval theologians like Aquinas of importing alien philosophy into the pure gospel of Christ. This didn't mean stripping the church of all traditions and practices not directly drawn from the Bible, though. Karlstadt adopted just such a rigorist position regarding things that were not drawn from the Bible during the time that Luther was at the Wartburg, and Luther emphatically refuted him. For Luther, there was no need to purify the church of non-Biblical elements. Nothing but what was found in the Bible should be taught as necessary for salvation, but many practices were simply indifferent.

Insistence on the Bible alone also did not, for Luther, mean that individuals could interpret the Bible any way they saw fit. Luther saw the dramatic consequences of allowing private interpretations of the Bible in the incident with the Zwickau prophets and in the Peasants' War. The ability to properly interpret scripture did not belong to the individual, but to the community as a whole.[6]

It is impossible to exaggerate how important the idea of *sola scriptura* was. If the Bible is the only legitimate source of religious authority, there follow all sorts of dramatic consequences. If the Bible alone has authority, then any man or woman who could read the Bible could be a theologian. This substantially limited the power of the church, since it could no longer authoritatively interpret the scripture for the masses.

It also contributed to growing support for education among the Protestants. Since the scripture was the key authority, available to every believer, it was vital that the masses should know how to read the Bible for themselves. Luther also assumed that people would be able to understand the Bible without complicated theological training. He favored the commonsense interpretation of difficult passages over the allegorical approach favored in medieval scholasticism. Such empowering of individuals foreshadows later developments in Western civilization. In fact, the historian Steven Ozment has claimed that "whatever else Protestantism was later to become [...] it is not too much to call the early Protestant movement the first Western enlightenment."[7]

5.1.3 The priesthood of all believers

If the Bible really is the sole authority for Christian doctrine, and if the individual Christian can have access to God without the mediation of the Church, this means a much more limited role for professional clergy in the Protestant world. Luther certainly did not seek to abolish the clergy, but he did argue that there was no essential difference between priests and laymen. Priests, for Luther, were not uniquely holy by virtue of their office, nor did they possess particular spiritual powers that were not available to non-priests. Instead, Luther taught that every Christian possessed the rights to forgive sins, to interpret scripture, and to test and judge doctrine. This idea came to be called the *priesthood of all believers*.

In the *Address to the Christian Nobility*, Luther argued that the German princes, by virtue of their legitimate Christian office as princes, should act as emergency bishops, since the actual bishops were not truly promoting the gospel.[8] Since there is no essential difference between priests and non-priests, this plan makes perfect sense. Similarly, the church was, for Luther, not the hierarchy and structure of the Catholic Church, but rather the gathered people of God.

Again, this idea had far-reaching consequences. If all believers belonged to what Luther called the "spiritual estate," this opened the door for priests to marry. Since, for Luther, priests were not set apart in some special way, there was no reason that they shouldn't live in the same way that others lived. Furthermore, it can be argued that the tenet of basic equality between people, which was assumed by the doctrine of the priesthood of all believers, contributed to the development of individual rights and democratic institutions in Europe. Derek Wilson, for example, argues that:

> If truth is the exclusive preserve of a priestly caste, any system built on this system will be autocratic. But, if truth is to be found in a book which anyone can read, then authority can be challenged with divine sanction. The way lies open for the development of alternative polities, even democracy.[9]

These, however, are long-term implications. Luther himself would certainly not have supported democracy or individual rights. But they do indicate just how significant the doctrine of the priesthood of all believers would become.

5.1.4 *The sacraments*

In *The Babylonian Captivity of the Church*, Luther criticized the Catholic position on the sacraments and reduced the number of sacraments to two—the Eucharist and Baptism.[10] Nevertheless, Luther's position on the sacraments was a good deal closer to the Catholic understanding than that of most other Protestants.[11] Many other Protestants—particularly the followers of Zwingli—understood the sacraments as symbols, but Luther insisted that they had real, actual effects.

For Luther, as for medieval Catholics, a sacrament was an external sign that signified an internal reality. This is something like the word *dog*—a sign—signifying the idea of a real dog. More powerfully, it is like the sign of a wedding ring signifying the reality of a marriage. The medieval church held that the sacraments are more powerful than these ordinary sorts of signs, though. Sacraments not only signify the grace of God, but actually confer that grace. Again, the metaphor of a marriage is helpful. The ceremony of a wedding not only symbolizes the marriage, but actually creates the state of marriage between the participants.

Because for Luther we cannot, on our own power, do anything to reconcile ourselves to God, we need to be changed from the outside. Something external needs to act upon us. For Luther, baptism and the Eucharist are the external things that act upon the believer to both symbolize and create the state of grace. But their action is not magical or automatic. Just as a wedding ceremony between unwilling participants will not create a real marriage, the sacraments are at some level dependent upon the faith of the participants.

In addition to the sign, Luther said, the sacrament must include a word from God. When the pastor speaks the words of the sacrament to the participant, it is the same as if God himself is speaking. So, when the pastor announces that your sins are forgiven, the participant can trust that God is actively declaring him forgiven. Since God cannot lie, believers can have absolute faith that the word declared through the sacrament is true. This gave the participants a level of confidence in God's grace that Luther had lacked as a young man. God, through the sacraments, has promised to save us, and on this promise we can rely.

5.1.5 Two kingdoms

Politically, Luther was conservative. His vigorous reaction to the social disorder that emerged from the 1525 Peasants' War demonstrated his respect for state and its social hierarchy. But the close relationship between church and state in late medieval Europe meant that Luther's rejection of the authority of the church necessarily meant that he had to reassess his understanding of civil authority as well.

At the Diet of Worms, Luther disobeyed the Emperor's command to recant, but he remained loyal to his own prince, Frederick the Wise. Many of the other German princes also supported Luther, but some opposed his teachings and persecuted his followers. Should the Protestants follow Romans 13, which counsels Christians to be subject to the governing authorities, or should they be willing to defy those authorities who sought to obstruct their faith or their access to the true gospel?

Luther resolved this dilemma by suggesting that humans were simultaneously part of two distinct kingdoms. Both kingdoms were ultimately ruled by God, but he ruled them in different ways. God rules the earthly kingdom by means of princes and earthly rulers. They govern their sphere through law, using physical force. The other kingdom—the heavenly—is ruled by means of the gospel and through grace. While all people are under the authority of secular rulers and under their laws, only true Christians, of whom Luther says there are few, are members of the heavenly kingdom. This means, though, that Christians have a kind of "dual citizenship," being subject to the laws of the earthly kingdom and to the gospel of the heavenly kingdom.[12]

This principle meant that Christians ought to be subject to secular authorities except when the government commands them to act contrary to the gospel. In that case, believers ought to obey God rather than human authority. Christians were, as dual citizens, allowed to fully participate in the activities of the state, including government and the military.

As the conflict between the Protestant princes and the Emperor grew during the 1520s and 1530s, Luther's political position subtly shifted. Early in his career, Luther had opposed any resistance to legitimate secular authority. At this point, he suggested that it was better for a Christian to be persecuted or even martyred than to rebel against the government that God had put into place. Gradually, however, Luther came to accept the legitimacy of Christians resisting the Emperor.[13]

Luther's political theology seems clearly to foreshadow many familiar elements in the modern world. Luther's division of two kingdoms may foreshadow the separation of church and state in modern western democracies. His ultimate defense of the right of resistance opened the door to the development of modern limited governments.

As Luther was processing and formulating these doctrines, life went on in Wittenberg. The reformed church that he was building grew and developed institutions, and Luther's personal life took a dramatic turn.

5.2 Marriage and Domestic Life

In the midst of the crises that Luther was working through in 1525, he did something astonishing. He got married. This move shocked and disturbed many of his friends, and scandalized the Catholic establishment. It also marked an important way in which the Protestants would diverge from traditional Catholicism.

Luther had long been thinking about the nature and the office of the clergy. He was particularly skeptical of doctrines like clerical celibacy and monastic vows that seemed to connect physical self-denial with greater spiritual merit. If we are justified by faith, Luther reasoned, we cannot improve our standing before God through monastic vows or clerical celibacy. So he began to question the value of these teachings.

He started slowly. In *The Address to the Christian Nobility*, he argued that priests should have the option to marry if they wished.[14] He added that most of those who made monastic vows failed to actually keep them. Furthermore, many under monastic vows had not voluntarily undertaken them, but had been forced to do so.[15] Later, in *The Babylonian Captivity*, he claimed that vows of celibacy are only tradition—and therefore not binding—since they are not mandated in the scriptures. Thus they cannot have any effect on the soul's salvation. They can only lead to pride.[16]

His criticisms of vows of celibacy proved to be far more popular than he expected. Monks and nuns began to leave their monasteries, citing Luther's influence. By 1521, the first priests began to marry, with Luther's approval. Luther himself, however, did not seem likely to marry. As late as November 1524, he wrote to Spalatin:

> Nevertheless, the way I feel now, and have felt thus far, I will not marry. It is not that I do not feel my flesh or sex, since I am neither wood nor stone, but my mind is far removed from marriage, since I daily expect death and the punishment due to a heretic. Therefore I shall not limit God's work in me, nor shall I rely on my own heart. Yet I hope God does not let me live long.[17]

Luther's bride, Katherine von Bora, was one of a group of nuns who had escaped from their convent, with Luther's help, and had arrived in Wittenberg to seek Luther's assistance in April 1523.[18] Katherine had entered the convent at the age of 10. Her family, though noble, was not wealthy and seems to have sent their daughter to the convent in order to relieve some financial pressure. While there, she received a good education and would later be able to converse capably in Latin with her husband.

After the nuns arrived in Wittenberg, Luther and his associates scrambled to find them all husbands. In the sixteenth century, when there were few opportunities for single women to live independently, this was a practical way to be sure that they were all safe and integrated into the community. It was also a way for Luther to emphasize his teachings on monastic vows. Katie and her companions had been forced into celibacy by their families, he reasoned. Their vows, therefore, could not be considered valid.

Luther attempted several times to find a husband for Katie, but to no avail. The first potential husband's family refused to allow their son to marry a runaway nun, and Katie herself rejected a second suitor. In a 1523 letter, she implied that she would accept Luther himself as a husband, but Luther did not seem interested at the time.[19] Ultimately, Luther, probably under some pressure from his followers to live by his stated principles, consented to marry Katie.

The marriage was sudden and took his friends almost completely by surprise. He informed his friends by letter:

> Thus I have now, according to the desire of my dear father, entered the marital estate. I have done so quickly lest bad tongues would stop it. Tuesday a week, which is Tuesday after St. John the Baptist, I am planning to have a small and joyful housewarming party. I did not want to hide this before you, my good friends and masters, and pray that we may have your blessing.[20]

Not everybody in Wittenberg was happy about his wedding. Melanchthon was offended, and wrote to a friend:

> On June 13, Luther unexpectedly and without informing any of his friends of what he was doing, married Bora […] You might be amazed that at this unfortunate time, when good and excellent men everywhere are in distress, he not only does not sympathize with them, but, as it seems, rather waxes wanton and diminishes his reputation, just when Germany has especial need of his judgment and authority.[21]

Perhaps because of this kind of reaction among his friends, Luther took care to explain his motives in some detail in a letter to his associate Nicholas Amsdorf:

> Indeed, the rumor is true that I was suddenly married to Catherine. [I did this] to silence the evil mouths which are so used to complaining against me. For I still hope to live for a little while. In addition, I also did not want to reject this unique [opportunity to obey] my father's wish for progeny, which he so often expressed. At the same time, I also wanted to confirm what I have taught by practicing it, for I find so many timid people in spite of such great light from the gospel.[22]

Luther's reasons for marrying Katie seem odd to us in the 21st century. He did not "fall in love" with Katie. Rather, he seems to have married more from a sense of duty than out of love. Indeed, later in his letter to Amsdorf, he admits that he felt "neither passionate love nor burning for my spouse, but I cherish her."[23] His friends seem to have hoped that marriage would help to smooth out some of the rough edges of Luther's personality, but this does not seem to have happened.[24] But, even though the marriage seems to have been initiated out of a sense of duty, the later correspondence between Luther and Katie indicates clearly that they came to love one another very deeply. Indeed, in 1531, he proudly proclaimed, "I wouldn't give up my Katy for France or for Venice."[25]

Luther's Catholic opponents were irate at the thought that Luther—who as an Augustinian monk had taken a vow of celibacy—would now presume to break that vow. The move was exaggerated by the fact that Katie, as a former nun, had also once taken a vow of celibacy. Henry VIII of England, whose own marital problems were just beginning to take shape, suggested that Luther had actually broken with the church simply because his lusts made him want to reject his monastic vows. Others had similar reactions, and Luther was left open to the charge that he had allowed his personal desires to influence his theological commitments.[26]

Despite all of this, the marriage was successful and set a lasting precedent for Protestants. The couple set up their household in the former Augustinian monastery, which the Elector had given to Luther. Katie managed the financial and domestic affairs of the household with skill and diligence, allowing Luther time to write and teach. They had six children, and remained happily married until Luther's death.

By marrying and raising a family, Luther did more than just demonstrate his commitment to his theology. He initiated a whole new attitude towards marriage. Celibacy was not God's highest calling anymore. Instead,

Luther taught that God had initiated marriage as a way for people to live in community on Earth. Luther's stand emphasized the importance of the family as the essential building block of society and lauded motherhood as a divine calling equal to any other. In the Protestant churches, the pastors would be involved in the normal world of relationships, child-rearing, and domestic affairs in which most people spent much of their lives. Thus, Protestant clergy came to live a life that much more closely mirrored those of their parishioners.

5.3 The Development of the Lutheran Church

The second half of the 1520s also saw the formal development of a distinctively Lutheran church organization, first in Saxony, and then spreading throughout Germany and eventually into Scandinavia and elsewhere. This development began with the accession of John the Steadfast as Elector of Saxony in 1525. Frederick the Wise, Luther's protector during the indulgence controversy, was a staunch defender of Luther, but his own religious beliefs were enigmatic. John, however, was a committed follower of Luther. As such, when he succeeded his brother, he began the process of formalizing a separate, specifically Lutheran ecclesiastical organization.

One of the important features of the new church organization was the active involvement of the prince in the administration of church affairs. This began as a purely practical move. Somebody responsible had to be in charge of things like distributing the property of the (now dissolved) monasteries. It developed into a system in which the administrative authority over church affairs, which had once been vested in the papacy and the church bureaucracy, was transferred to the state.

With John's encouragement, and recognizing that his differences with the Catholic Church were too great to be resolved anytime soon, Luther began to make changes to the organization of the Saxon church and to its order of worship. He moved cautiously, being unwilling to make dramatic changes or to needlessly abolish ceremonies or rituals. In his first revised liturgy for the church in Wittenberg, published in 1523, he claimed to have made no innovations, declaring "I have been hesitant and fearful, partly because of the weak in faith, who cannot suddenly exchange an old and accustomed order of worship for a new and unusual one."[27]

The church in Electoral Saxony was directly affected by Luther's changes, but the Saxon church soon became a model for Protestant churches in other territories. Elector John wholeheartedly supported Luther, providing both money and political support to bolster Luther's initiatives. John's support of Luther's reforming efforts helped cement the growing role of the secular lords in the church. The church structures that John and Luther began to develop were largely an attempt to bring order and consistency to the Saxon church.

John organized a series of visitations, in which Luther and other Protestant leaders traveled throughout Saxony to investigate the state of the churches. What they found was not encouraging. Many local priests did not know the basics of the Christian faith, and others did not live up to the moral standards that they had been preaching. In the aftermath of these visitations, Luther and his associates—along with the Elector—began to develop a system of oversight for the churches and for proper instruction in the basics of the Protestant faith for the clergy.

One element of this instruction was the publication of two catechisms— short instructional works designed to easily teach regular people the basics of the faith. Luther had been working on the catechisms for several years, and the work culminated in 1529 with the publication of the *Large* and *Small Catechisms*.[28] Both of these were short textbooks that contained basic questions about the Protestant faith, and short, easily memorized answers. The idea was that, by memorizing the material in the catechism, people would come to understand and internalize the main elements of Protestant doctrine. The *Large Catechism* was written to instruct pastors and teachers. The less detailed *Small Catechism* was for use by the common people, and especially for training small children in the basics of the faith. It contained Luther's brief explanations of the Ten Commandments, the Lord's Prayer, and the Apostles' Creed, along with some material on the nature of the sacraments. The *Small Catechism* is one of Luther's most enduring works, still commonly used in Lutheran churches to this day. He considered it, along with his *Bondage of the Will*, to be one of his two most important works.[29]

The new church also needed a new form for worship. Luther wanted to remove any impediments to the congregation's understanding of the gospel message. He was thus in favor of removing much of the Latin from the service, so that the congregation, most of whom did not know the scholarly language, could understand what was going on. He was also concerned to purge the church service of those elements of the Catholic mass that he now considered to be false teaching. But he did not want to radically change the service, both because he respected many elements of the traditional mass, and because he did not want the people to be shocked and disturbed by too much change at once.

Luther's first liturgy was published in 1523.[30] The hymns were sung in German, but much of the rest of the service was still in Latin. An important change was that during the Eucharist, the parishioners received both the bread and the wine, against the traditional Catholic practice of serving the laity only the bread. But Luther slowly introduced more substantial changes.

By 1526, Luther initiated the first fully German mass.[31] The form was still similar to the traditional Catholic service, but the German language was used throughout. Some Catholic elements that had been rejected by other, more radical reformers such as Zwingli were still present in Luther's German Mass, including the elevation of the host at the Eucharist and the optional use of special vestments for the clergy. Nevertheless, there was still freedom for individual congregations to adjust and alter the order of service for their own particular needs. The 1526 mass also included the congregational singing of hymns, something that was uncommon in Catholic churches before the Reformation, but which Luther would give pride of place in his liturgical theology.

5.4 Music

Music in church is one of Luther's most significant impacts on Christian worship. In the middle ages, congregations rarely sang. Luther insisted, on the other hand, that singing together was an essential part of worship. He exuberantly praised music as being able to accomplish things that words alone could not.

> Next to the Word of God, music deserves the highest praise [...] For whether you wish to comfort the sad, to terrify the happy, to encourage the despairing, to humble the proud, to calm the dispassionate, or to appease those full of hate [...] what more effective means than music could you find?[32]

Luther himself was an extraordinarily talented musician, and his contributions to church music are substantial. He played the lute well, and often accompanied his family in after-dinner singing. He had a fine tenor voice, and a talent for writing hymns. His emphasis on the importance of quality music in worship was unique among the early reformers, many of whom were suspicious of any practice that evoked the ritualism of the Catholic mass.

In contrast to the professional choirs employed by Catholic churches, Luther strove to include the entire congregation in singing. He also employed vernacular languages rather than Latin. He was disappointed with the quality of the German hymns that were available to him, so he composed many of his own and challenged the poetically talented among his congregation to write hymns as well.[33]

Luther saw music as both a vehicle for proclaiming the gospel and as a special gift given to humans by God. One of his most lasting compositions is the hymn *A Mighty Fortress*, which Luther based on the text of Psalm 46, and which is still regularly sung in Protestant churches today. In fact, many people who know little about Luther are still familiar with his hymns.

Taken all together, the reforms that Luther made during the 1520s are staggering. He formulated a new way of thinking about how people can be reconciled with God. But he also introduced new ways to think about marriage and the family, a new form for congregational worship, and new kinds of relationships between church and state.

Chapter 6

THE FINAL YEARS

6.1 Home Life

Luther lived for 20 years after his marriage, and these last 20 years of his life are often neglected by biographers. There are several reasons for the relative neglect of Luther's later years. In part it has to do with the fact that, while Luther's life was exciting in the 1520s, the 1530s were a less eventful time. The excitement of the years in which he broke with the church, married, reprimanded the peasants and quarreled with friends and foes over doctrine gave way to a slower, more stable life for Luther. It is also challenging, especially for admirers of Luther, to tell the story of his later years because Luther grew increasingly quarrelsome as he got older. In the 1530s and 1540s he produced a number of increasingly violent treatises against those whom he saw as the enemies of the gospel. Despite this, the last 20 years of his life are important to give us a full picture of who Luther was.

Unlike the relative obscurity of his early years, Luther was a major public figure in the 1530s and was well known throughout Europe. As such, he often received visitors in Wittenberg from throughout Europe. One of these travelers has left us a remarkable firsthand description of a visit with Luther in 1523. This text gives a strong sense of Luther's personality and lifestyle, and is worth quoting at length:

> Luther conveys the same impression in his countenance as in his books. His eyes are penetrating and they almost sparkle in a sinister fashion as one can observe it at times among the mentally ill [...] His manner of speech is vehement, abounding in insinuations and ridicule. His apparel hardly distinguishes him from a courtier. When he leaves the house in which he lives—it was formerly the cloister—he wears, it is said, the robe of his order. Sitting together with him we did not merely talk but

also drank beer and wine in a good mood, as is the custom there. In every respect he seems to be a "good fellow," as they say in German. The integrity of his life, which is frequently praised among us here, does not distinguish him from the rest of us. Easily one can recognize his arrogance and presumptuousness. Slander, calumny and ridicule seem to be a part of him. His books point this out clearly. It is said that he is well-read and that he writes much.[1]

The author seems suspicious of Luther, yet cannot help but acknowledge that he was gregarious and intelligent. This description expresses the enigmatic nature of Luther as a person. He could be a friendly companion and a well-read scholar, but also, at the same time, coarse and arrogant. These characteristics aptly represent the last years of Luther's life.

After their marriage, Luther and Katie quickly settled into their new home in Wittenberg. The elector had given them the former Augustinian monastery in which Luther had lived as a monk, and they transformed it into a comfortable home. While Katie managed the household, Luther was able to continue his work at the university. He lectured regularly on various biblical texts. He continued to work on his German translation of the Bible, the full text of which appeared in 1534. He was appointed dean of the university in 1535, from which position he helped to reorganize the university curriculum in 1536. He also remained busy with writing and preaching and continued to be involved, mostly through published treatises, in the various theological controversies of the day.

Much of his life, however, was taken up with his family. Luther and Katie had six children, four of whom lived to adulthood. His first daughter, Elizabeth, died at just eight months. Losing Elizabeth was difficult for Luther, but when his daughter Magdalene died in 1542 at the age of 13, he was devastated. In a conversation with his students, he reflected on the tension between his assurance that Magdalene's suffering was over and that she was united with God in heaven, and his own deep grief over losing his beloved daughter:

> I am joyful in spirit but I am sad according to the flesh. The flesh doesn't take kindly to this. The separation [caused by death] troubles me above measure. It is strange to know that she is surely at peace and that she is well off there, and yet to grieve so much.[2]

This picture of Luther as a grieving father, struggling to reconcile his beliefs with his emotions, gives us a rare glimpse into the humanness of a historic figure. And Luther came to see family life, with its joys and heartbreaks, as a vital part of the Christian life. This was something the pope, committed as he was to clerical celibacy, simply could not understand. Luther knew the joys of a child's first steps and the grief of a child's early death. And he felt that experiencing these things made him a more effective pastor and leader. He was happy to have the children near him while he worked. He was also known to set aside his dignity and play with them enthusiastically.

In addition to Katie and the children, the Luther household included a number of servants and several relatives. The family also often took in university students as boarders. After dinner, the family would often gather together for music, accompanied by Luther on his lute. He loved to play chess and skittles with the children and with guests.[3] It was a bustling household, made more so by the students who frequented the house to study with Luther or to take meals with the family.

Students often ate in the houses of their professors in Wittenberg, as was customary in sixteenth-century universities. The esteem in which these students held Luther explains the popularity of his table with the university students, and the fact that several of these students took detailed notes of the proceedings around the table. These notes have come down to us as the *Table Talk*. The *Table Talk* shows us the human side of Luther far more than do his own published works. In them we see Luther teaching theology and dispensing wise advice, but we also see his bursts of anger and his love for crass humor. These are a rich source of insight into Luther, and from them we get a more complete picture of Luther—warts and all—than we have from any other person from his era. To be sure, the nature of the *Table Talk*—that they are student notes taken at impromptu gatherings—means that scholars have to use them carefully. Nevertheless, they give us a valuable insight into Luther's later life.

6.2 Physical and Emotional Illnesses

As the *Table Talk* testifies, Luther could be grumpy and intolerant. As he grew older, these traits seem to have become more pronounced. This is perhaps why his admirers are less comfortable with the older Luther than with the reformer of the 1520s. But Luther had always been a rather angry man, a trait that he himself acknowledged. He reflected:

> I was born to war with fanatics and devils. Thus my books are very stormy and bellicose. I must root out the stumps and trunks, hew away the thorns and briar, fill in the puddles. I am the coarse woodsman, who must pioneer and hew a path.[4]

It was also a trait which his friends often found difficult to bear. But his anger grew and became more bitter as he aged. Many of his most aggressive and polarizing works were written after 1530. This coincides with a general decline in Luther's health during the last years of his life.

Luther had never been a particularly healthy man. He had experienced bouts of illness throughout his life. Some of this can be traced to his lifestyle. Remember that he spent much of his early adulthood enduring the self-denial of the monastery. After he left the monastic life and married, his habits moved to the other extreme, and he enjoyed good food and drink rather heavily. He was regularly tormented by gallstones and kidney problems. He also wrote regularly of headaches, ringing in the ears, and other similar ailments.

He tended to associate these physical ailments with spiritual struggles and often understood his physical discomforts to be attacks of the devil, or as reminders sent by God to keep him humble. This is the sort of language that makes some modern readers uncomfortable, and some have asked whether this might be evidence that Luther was suffering from mental as well as physical health problems.[5] But psychological health is far more difficult to measure than physical health, especially in a man who lived 500 years ago. It seems unlikely that there could be enough evidence available to modern researchers to make any definitive statement about Luther's mental health. In any event, despite his ailments, he remained remarkably productive right up to his death.

It is also sometimes suggested that his illnesses may have contributed to the increasing bitterness that characterized Luther's later years. Although one cannot attribute all of Luther's polemical excesses to ill health, it seems reasonable to draw some connection between his health issues and his growing anger.[6]

6.3 Polemics and Controversies

One of the noticeable features of Luther's writings is the fact that he seemed to have little patience for those with whom he disagreed. Thus he had a tendency, throughout his career, to write angry, polemical treatises against anybody whom he saw as standing in the way of God's work. In addition to the papacy and the Catholic Church, which were favorite targets throughout his career, Luther also wrote angrily against fellow Protestants who disagreed with him on matters of doctrine or practice. Perhaps most troublingly, Luther wrote some scathing tracts attacking the non-Christian communities in Europe. This tendency to bitterly attack his opponents accelerated during the last years of his life. The growing vitriol may be related to his deteriorating health, but may also be due to the fact that Luther seems to have become increasingly convinced that the end of the world and the final judgment were at hand.[7]

One common theme in Luther's polemics is his insistence on the Gospel. His attacks on the Pope, on Zwingli, on the Zwickau prophets, on the Jews and on the Turks all revolve around Luther's conviction that these groups, by refusing to accept the Protestant gospel, were somehow impeding God's work on earth. He seems to have seen Catholics, Jews and Muslims all as trying to earn salvation through their own efforts and, by doing so, undermining the vital gospel of justification by faith alone. In a 1537 sermon, Luther made this very point:

> The Turk, the pope, and the Jews depict God as an angry God, but as one whose anger can be allayed and whose favor can be won if I humble myself, fast, sacrifice, perform good works, and expiate my sins with an ascetic life.[8]

So while his polemical tracts—especially those concerning the Jews—contain much that is reprehensible, we should remember that his antipathy toward his opponents was not racial, but religious.

6.3.1 Islam and the Turks

Luther's writings about Islam are clearly colored by the fact that in the sixteenth century it was so closely associated with the military advances of the Ottoman Empire. The *Table Talk* often records Luther talking with his students about the latest military developments in the Balkans. Luther associated the growth of Turkish power with God's judgments on Catholic rulers like the emperor for their persecution of the Protestants.[9] He recognized that the Turkish invasions of southern Europe were dangerous, and he supported military action against the Ottomans to stop their advance into Europe. But he also worried that the emperor's military buildup, which was ostensibly to defend against the Turkish invasion, might also be used to crush the Protestants. Luther opposed carrying out any sort of crusade or holy war against Islam. Instead he viewed the military actions against the Turks as a war of self-defense against an aggressive enemy.[10]

As for Islam itself, it seems likely that Luther had limited understanding of Muslim doctrine and practices, although he apparently saw a Latin translation of the Koran in 1542.[11] Luther tended to see Islam as teaching a kind of works-righteousness that he opposed in any form. So he assumed that Muslims are trying to merit God's favor by their own efforts. As such, Islam directly opposed the gospel of justification by faith alone.[12]

6.3.2 The question of the Jews

Few of Luther's polemical writings are as well known or as troubling as his later writings against the Jews. Luther advocated a level of violence against the Jews that cannot be ignored. And, particularly in light of the horrific events of the twentieth century, we must unequivocally repudiate these writings. Nevertheless, we should remember that Luther was a man of his age and that his writings about the Jews are more complex than they may initially seem.

In fact, Luther's first major treatise on Judaism was largely a defense of the Jews. In *That Jesus Christ Was Born a Jew* (1523), Luther reminded his German readers of the important connections between Judaism and Christianity.[13] The treatise is mostly a criticism of scholastic theologians, whom Luther saw as denying Christ's true humanity. He hoped that the Jews would convert to Protestant Christianity, but he suggested that compassion and tolerance were better ways to encourage their conversion than violence and persecution. He was particularly critical of the way that church authorities had treated Jews up to that time. If the church adopted a more tolerant attitude, he reasoned, more Jews might convert to Christianity. "If I had been a Jew and had seen such dolts and blockheads govern and teach the Christian faith," he wrote, "I would sooner have become a hog than a Christian."[14] This treatise gave Luther a reputation in the 1520s as being relatively sympathetic toward the Jews.

Initially, it was just this pro-Jewish reputation that led to Luther's more well-known anti-Semitic treatises of the 1530s. In 1536, Elector John Frederick, who had succeeded his father as elector of Saxony in 1532, issued a decree expelling the Jews from Saxony and forbidding them even to travel through his territory. In and of itself, this was not unusual in the sixteenth century. But it did attract criticism. A prominent Jewish scholar, Josel of Rosheim, wrote to Luther in 1537, using the well-known Hebrew scholar Wolfgang Capitio as intermediary. Rosheim seems to have assumed, based on Luther's previous writings, that Luther was relatively friendly toward the Jewish people and could use his influence with the elector to have the decree repealed. This letter propelled Luther into action.

His response was bitter. The Jews, he wrote, could only relieve their suffering by accepting Christ and his gospel. Luther may have been frustrated that his earlier, more tolerant attitude toward the Jews had not encouraged them to convert to Protestantism. He wrote angrily to Rosheim: "For the sake of the crucified Jew, whom no one will take from me, I gladly wanted to do my best for you Jews, except that you abused my favor and hardened your hearts."[15] An item in the *Table Talk* further illustrates this harsh response. Upon receiving Rosheim's letter, Luther is reported to have exclaimed, "Why should we give permission to those rascals who injure people in body and property and with their superstitions cause many Christians to fall away?"[16] He was apparently referring to rumors that Jews in Moravia had been forcibly circumcising Christians. This rumor and others like it circulated through Germany in the sixteenth century. There was no factual basis for them, of course, but Luther, along with many others, accepted them as true. This may help to explain Luther's growing animosity toward the Jews. But it seems likely that the primary factor was Luther's disappointment that Jews were not, as he had hoped, converting to Protestantism.

Luther released a still more vicious attack on the Jews some years later, in 1543. In *On the Jews and Their Lies*, Luther viciously attacked the Jews for refusing to accept Christ as the Messiah and for spreading teachings that might lead people away from the gospel.

> They turned a deaf ear to us in the past and still do so, although many fine scholarly people, including some from their own race, have refuted them so thoroughly that even stone and wood, if endowed with a particle of reason, would have to yield. Yet they rave consciously against recognized truth. Their accursed rabbis, who indeed know better, wantonly poison the minds of their poor youth and of the common man and divert them from the truth.[17]

Luther's concern here is religious, but it is not racial. He is frustrated that the Jews refuse to accept a gospel that is—to him—a self-evident truth. He is angry that they continue to hold on to doctrines that—in his view—have been refuted. Worst of all, he is frightened that their teachings might impede the spread of the gospel.

Thus, Luther proposed a series of cruel policies designed to purify Christian Germany from the dangerous teachings of the Jews. He believed their houses should be knocked down, their synagogues burned, their religious texts confiscated, and their rabbis forbidden to teach. They should not be allowed to travel or trade, and should be forced into manual labor.[18] In this way, Luther hoped to prevent the Jews from harming Christians or impeding the spread of the gospel. Somehow, Luther's attitude toward the Jews had shifted. Where he had once seen them as fellow human beings and potential converts, he now seemed to see them as dangerous enemies.

We must, in no uncertain terms, repudiate Luther on this. For one thing, his tirade against the Jews was fueled, at least in part, by false accusations against the German Jews that Luther took to be true. But more importantly, Luther's call for violent measures against the Jews falls into the same trap that he had accused the Catholics of in *That Jesus Christ Was Born a Jew*.

Luther had earlier recognized that violent force was not only un-Christian, but ineffective.[19]

But we should also resist the temptation to link Luther's anti-Semitism with the vicious racialism of the twentieth century. The claim that Luther's teachings somehow led to Nazi racial policies is unsustainable.[20]

We also need to remember to look at Luther's anti-Semitic tracts in context. Luther was, without question, vicious toward the Jews. But he was also vicious (and with a similar level of venom) toward the papacy and even toward fellow Protestants with whom he disagreed on some point of doctrine. And it is worth pointing out that anti-Semitism was relatively widespread in Germany during the sixteenth century. Even otherwise moderate figures like Erasmus occasionally engaged in anti-Semitic tirades. But this does not excuse Luther's advocacy of violence, nor can we explain it away. Instead, we would do well to remember that even great men can be deeply flawed, and that even bitter and angry men can change the world for the better.

6.3.3 *Philip of Hesse and bigamy*

Another odd incident in Luther's later life was his involvement with the bigamous second marriage of Landgrave Philip of Hesse. This strange event proved embarrassing to Luther, and illustrates some of the ways in which the nascent Protestant movement had to come to terms with the practical implications of its theological commitments.

Philip of Hesse was perhaps the most important early political champion of Protestantism. He was an early convert and enthusiastic supporter of Luther and his fellow reformers. His support for the Protestants was indispensable in the 1520s. His main goal was to unify the various Protestants into a cohesive group that could effectively resist the emperor and the papacy. It was Philip, for instance, who organized the Marburg Colloquy between Luther and Zwingli in 1525. He was thus in a position to demand some of Luther's attention for his personal problems. And this is just what Philip did in 1539, when he asked Luther for a judgment on his marriage.

Philip's chief problem was his wife. He deeply disliked her. But the marriage was a political one, linking Hesse and Saxony, so he couldn't simply divorce her. Adding to his troubles was the fact that Philip was apparently an honestly religious man, and he worried that extramarital affairs, such as he had engaged in before his conversion to Protestantism, might put his soul in jeopardy. But he felt that he couldn't live with his wife any longer, and he wasn't the sort of man who was willing to adopt a celibate lifestyle. So he asked Luther whether, instead of divorcing his wife and remarrying, it might be acceptable to simply marry a second wife.

This was a risky plan. Bigamy was a capital offense in the Holy Roman Empire. But, Luther had already broken with many traditional teachings on marriage, so Philip hoped that he might be willing to move another step away from traditional marriage. Furthermore, the Old Testament was replete with examples of divinely sanctioned polygamous marriages. If the Bible was our doctrinal foundation, Philip reasoned, wasn't it reasonable to assume that polygamy could be a legitimate option? It is also likely that Philip was aware that Luther had suggested, when asked about the case of Henry VIII and his request for a divorce, that Henry would be better off marrying a second wife than divorcing.[21]

In response to Philip's inquiry, Luther, along with his fellow reformers Philip Melanchthon and Martin Bucer, advised him that the best course of action would be to content himself to live a chaste and monogamous life with his wife. But they left open the possibility that, in extraordinary circumstances, bigamy might be allowable. This was all the permission Philip needed, and he married a second wife soon after receiving the reformers' advice.

The second marriage, although supposed to be secret, was publicly known almost as soon as it happened. Luther seems to have been a bit embarrassed that he was implicated in the scandal, although he stubbornly refused to admit any wrongdoing. For Philip, the bigamy was a terrible political miscalculation. Since bigamy was a serious crime, it gave the emperor the leverage he needed to destabilize Philip's Protestant alliance. Philip hastily signed a treaty in which the emperor agreed to overlook Philip's bigamy in exchange for substantial political concessions that would weaken the Protestants for years to come. It was less of a disaster for Luther personally, but his involvement allowed his enemies to accuse him of debasing the institution of marriage.

The affair surrounding Philip's bigamy illustrates some of the difficult questions that Luther and the Protestants were working out in the 1530s. Philip's political position was certainly an issue, which raised the question of the extent to which political leaders who supported the Protestants could expect to influence doctrinal discussions. More substantially, it raised the question of how far the Protestants were willing to go in their reforms of moral practice. Bigamy, they ultimately decided, was one step too far.

6.4 The End

Despite his illnesses and the controversies swirling about him, Luther worked hard until the very end of his life. He continued to teach, to write and to preach regularly until the very moment of his death. He was very concerned about the future of the German Protestants, and put as much effort as he could muster into supporting the pastors and congregations in Saxony. In

1543, three years before his death, he wrote to his friend Wenceslaus Link that even though he felt more dead than alive and was overwhelmed with work, nevertheless "I do not leave our congregations in poor shape; they flourish in pure and sound teaching, and they grow day by day through many excellent and most sincere pastors."[22]

It is particularly fitting that Luther should end his life in the same city as he began it. Count Albrecht III of Mansfield, Luther's birthplace, had been involved in a lengthy and complicated quarrel with various family members, which the count had asked Luther to help mediate. Furthermore, Luther was concerned by reports coming out of Mansfield that the count, although a dutiful supporter of the Reformation, was an unjust and oppressive ruler. Luther felt bound by his historic ties to Mansfield and agreed to advise the count and to serve as arbitrator in his disputes with his relatives. In this role, Luther traveled several times to Mansfield and maintained a robust correspondence with the count.

His final trip began in January 1546. He set out for Eisleben, the capital of Mansfield, with several companions, including three of his sons. The journey from Wittenberg took a week, since the party was delayed for several days by a flooding river. Shortly after their arrival in Eisleben, Luther suffered a fainting spell. Although his companions were alarmed, Luther brushed it off. He wrote to Katie that she need not worry about him. The dizziness, he claimed, was his own fault. He even teased her by saying that he was well enough to be tempted by beautiful women![23]

He spent the next two weeks preaching in Mansfield and working with the count. He found the task somewhat distasteful and wrote to Katie that he would be relieved when it was finally over.[24] His letters home were filled with calls for Katie not to worry about his health and safety. The following sample gives a strong sense of Luther's personality:

> For you prefer to worry about me instead of letting God worry, as if he were not almighty and could not create ten Doctor Martins, should the old one drown in the Saale, or burn in the oven, or perish in Wolfgang's bird trap. Free me from your worries. I have a caretaker who is better than you and all the angels; he lies in the cradle and rests upon a virgin's bosom, and yet, nevertheless, he sits at the right hand of God, the almighty Father. Therefore be at peace.[25]

He preached his final sermon on February 15, finishing early with the words, "I am too weak and will let it go at that."[26] The next day the negotiations with the count were satisfactorily concluded. After signing the final documents, Luther began to have chest pains. He lay down in his room and his friends summoned doctors and a pharmacist. They could not help him. He died, surrounded by friends and companions, between 2:00 and 3:00 in the morning of February 18.

Luther's last written words were found scribbled on a note in his pocket:

> Nobody can understand Virgil in his Bucolics and Georgics unless he has first been a shepherd or a farmer for five years. Nobody understands Cicero in his letters unless he has been engaged in public affairs of some consequence for twenty years. Let nobody suppose that he has tasted the Holy Scriptures sufficiently unless he has ruled over the churches with the prophets for a hundred years. Therefore there is something wonderful, first, about John the Baptist; second, about Christ; third, about the apostles. "Lay not your hand on this divine Aeneid, but bow before it, adore its every trace." We are beggars. That is true.[27]

These words can be seen as a kind of final testament. They illustrate the final thoughts of a man who had profoundly changed the world, but who also recognized his own limitations and weaknesses.

When the elector heard of Luther's death, he immediately sent for the body and began planning for a grand funeral in the Castle Church—the same church where Luther had posted the 95 Theses almost thirty years before. A funeral procession formed, and the body slowly made its way back to Wittenberg. The mourners stopped several times along the way for various eulogies and for the public to mourn. When the procession arrived at Wittenberg, the whole town turned out for the funeral.

Philip Melanchthon gave the eulogy. In it, he presented Luther as the latest in a great succession of prophets, apostles and church fathers who were called to bring God's word to the people. As such, Luther stood in line with great figures like the prophet Jeremiah, St. Paul, and Bernard of Clairvaux. Melanchthon expressed the Protestant community's deep admiration for Luther:

> We justly grieve for our own sake that such a man—endowed with the greatest powers of intellect, versed in doctrine, trained by long practice, adorned with many outstanding and heroic virtues, chosen by God for the renewal of the church, and who furthermore embraced us all in his fatherly heart—has been called from among us. For we closely resemble orphans who have lost an outstanding and faithful father.[28]

He did not ignore Luther's rough edges, citing Erasmus's saying that "because of the greatness of its diseases God gave this final age a severe physician."[29]

After the funeral, Luther was laid to rest beneath the pulpit of the Castle Church, a fitting location for the grave of a man who did much of his greatest work as a preacher.

The reformer Martin Bucer, who had come under Luther's influence at the Heidelberg Disputation in 1518, and who led the reform movement in Strasbourg, wrote to a friend upon hearing of Luther's death:

> I know how many people hate Luther. And yet the fact remains: God loved him very much and never gave us a holier and more effective instrument of the Gospel. Luther had shortcomings, in fact serious ones. But God bore them and put up with them, never granting another mortal a mightier spirit and such divine power to proclaim His Son and to strike down the Antichrist. If God so accepted him and drew him near to Himself, in spite of his being a sinner—a sinner, of course, who abhorred evil like no other—who am I, a wretched servant and miserable sinner who shows so little zeal in pursuing justice, to reject him and turn him down on account of his failings, which we, of course, should not condone? Do we not often ask others to tolerate even greater failings in ourselves?[30]

Bucer's analysis seems an appropriate way to sum up Luther's life. He was a controversial figure and not always an easy man to love. But his impact was immense, and our criticism of his failings, however great they may be, cannot undermine the tremendous value of his positive achievements.

Luther's death, of course, was not the end of his influence. Indeed, few men have had such an enormous influence after their death as did the reformer of Wittenberg.

Chapter 7

THE WORLD LUTHER MADE

7.1 Long-Term Impacts

Although Luther lived nearly five hundred years ago, his influence can still be clearly felt in the twenty-first century. His actions and ideas changed Western civilization in profound ways, and the world in which we live is, in many ways, built upon the foundation that Luther laid. The historian A. G. Dickens summarized the enduring impact of Luther's reformation, despite the distance and foreignness of his context:

> When we have finished bewailing the greed, folly and fanaticism of the sixteenth century, the Reformation still stands in mountainous bulk across the landscapes of western Christianity. It concerned most issues which still live to perplex and divide us.[1]

Dickens is quite correct; Luther's legacy looms large in the twenty-first century. And this legacy is felt not only through the churches that Luther and his followers founded. Indeed, many of the major aspects of Western civilization—the growth of individualism, the rise of the nation state, and the development of public education, among others—can be traced to key ideas developed by Luther.

7.1.1 *The spread of Lutheranism*

Some parts of Luther's legacy are quite easy to observe. The proliferation of churches that trace their heritage to Luther's reformation is an example. Today there are more than sixty million people in the world who affiliate with churches that bear the name Lutheran, all of which, to one degree or another, continue to affirm Luther's theology. And even though Lutheranism itself remained largely within its homeland of northern Europe, Luther's influence is also felt in the growth of various other forms of Protestantism worldwide. Baptists, Presbyterians, Methodists and other Protestant denominations each developed their own unique take on Luther's theological insights. This makes more than eight hundred million people in the world today whose religious heritage can be traced directly to Luther's actions and ideas.

Lutheranism itself rapidly grew in the sixteenth century. Saxony and many other north German states quickly adopted Lutheranism as their state religion during Luther's lifetime. From there, his ideas spread northward into Scandinavia.[2] Many Swedish and Danish students studied under Luther and his associates at Wittenberg. In fact, literature's most famous Dane— Shakespeare's Hamlet—was a student at Wittenberg. When these students returned to their homelands, they brought Luther's ideas with them. Sweden is an instructive example.

Two Swedish brothers, Olaus and Laurentius Petri, were students of Luther and Melanchthon at Wittenberg in the early 1520s. After they returned home to Sweden, they began to preach Luther's Protestant gospel. While local church officials initially opposed the pair, they ultimately found a powerful supporter in the new Swedish king, Gustavus Vasa, who had successfully led Sweden to independence from the Danish king Christian II in 1523. Vasa may have been attracted by Lutheran theology, but he was also quite aware of the fact that, as a Protestant king, he was likely to have much more authority over religious matters in Sweden than he would as a Catholic. Like in Germany, religious and political motivations were closely intertwined. In 1527, Vasa officially proclaimed Sweden to be a Protestant country.

Similar reform movements happened in Denmark, Norway, Iceland, and Finland, each of which adopted Lutheranism as their official state religion during the sixteenth century. From there, Lutheranism moved to the United States, largely with the German and Scandinavian immigrants who flocked to the New World during the nineteenth and twentieth centuries. European colonialism brought Lutheranism to Africa, where today some of the largest Lutheran churches in the world can be found in Tanzania, Ethiopia and Madagascar.

Beyond the specifically Lutheran churches, the Protestant movements in Switzerland, England, Holland and Scotland all developed, at least partially, out of Luther's teachings. By the end of the sixteenth century, half of Europe had adopted some form of Protestantism. All of these movements can point to Luther as an influence.

But Luther's legacy is far from limited to the growth of the churches that he helped to found. A more important part of his legacy can be seen in the impact of his ideas on society. The key ideas that Luther defended—justification by faith, the authority of scripture and the priesthood of all believers—were a bit like a Pandora's Box. Once these ideas had been unleashed, they could not be contained, and they spread beyond their original intentions. So while Luther himself would not have supported things like individual liberty or women's rights, those modern concepts can be seen as developing out of his ideas.

7.1.2   The growth of individualism

A lot of the forces that Luther set into motion in the sixteenth century continue to have powerful influences on Western society. One of the most significant of these is the growth of individualism. Scholars often note that Luther's thought may have contributed—albeit unintentionally—to the idea of the sovereign individual. Thus Derek Wilson, in his recent biography of Luther, suggested that:

> Luther's revolution was a very limited one: he intended to return the church to its New Testament doctrines. What he actually did, without realizing it, was to provide oxygen to human individualism.[3]

And Martin Marty, in an interview about Luther's influence, remarked that Luther was "the greatest single agent in increasing the value of the individual."[4]

What do these writers mean when they connect Luther with individualism? Certainly Luther himself did not consciously promote individualism. Indeed, his conviction that the human will was bound and his firm belief that human beings are not capable of affecting their own salvation might seem to argue against the value of the individual. Nevertheless, his firm insistence on the priesthood of all believers, his call for people to read the Bible for themselves, and his rejection of any authorities outside of the Bible and his own conscience all served to emphasize the value and the ability of the individual.

Individualism can be both a blessing and a curse. It is likely to be an attractive idea to modern students who presumably see clearly the benefits of individualism—the fact that individuals can be empowered to take greater control of their own lives, for instance. By rejecting the institutional power of the church and by encouraging individuals to read the Bible for themselves, Protestant theology implied that no person or institution had the right to tell anybody else what to believe or how to understand the Bible. To be clear, Luther himself would reject the idea that individuals have the right to believe anything that they wish. In his mind, there was a true gospel, to which each individual believer needed to be subject. But the seeds of such an idea are plausibly connected to Luther's teachings.

There are also drawbacks to a growing focus on the individual. Luther's opponents may have seen this connection more clearly than Luther did, as many of them explicitly connected Luther's teachings with the breakdown of social order. The growing power of the individual stood in tension with the shared social mores that held society together. In order for society to function, there must be some sort of generally acknowledged authority to bind the community together. As the authority of the individual conscience came to overshadow the religious authority of the church, there was little to stop the community from fragmenting into ever smaller groups. And this is precisely what happened within Protestantism. Ultimately, the power of the state would have to step in to restore social order. But the religious uniformity of pre-Reformation Europe was lost forever.

One undeniable result of Luther's break with the church was thus the tendency for Protestants to continue to break from one another over ever smaller issues of doctrine and practice. Once the Pandora's Box of reform had been cracked open by Luther, there was little to prevent others from breaking with their church over their own understanding of the Bible. From here, there was no return. The modern world would grow increasingly pluralistic, in the sense that there would grow to be more and more different ways for people to answer basic questions about God and theology. And Western society would adapt and allow individuals to choose their own way among these various religious paths. So Luther's teachings seem—unintentionally—to have contributed to modern individualism.

7.1.3 *Nationalism and politics*

Luther was also deeply influential in the realm of politics and statecraft. His influence here, however, is enigmatic. In some ways, Luther's ideas encouraged German nationalism and contributed to the development of strong, centralized states and absolute monarchies. In other ways, Luther's advocacy of the individual conscience may be seen as having laid the groundwork for the modern liberal state. In any case, Luther left a lasting mark on politics.

Luther's political thought began with the assumption that God had given rulers their office and that rebellion against those divinely appointed rulers was tantamount to rebellion against God. So Luther tended to support the power of the state. He was deeply concerned about social disorder and fearful of anarchy.[5] His experiences in the early 1520s with Karlstadt's radical reforms and especially with the disorder related to the Peasants' War in 1525 drove home for him the negative consequences of social disorder and led him to support a strong government. So, in the 1520s, Luther was a staunch defender of the state, seeing it as the only thing preventing anarchy from overtaking the world.[6] He was even initially uncomfortable with using military force to defend the Protestant princes against imperial attempts to reassert Catholicism since the emperor was, after all, a divinely appointed ruler. As time went on, however, Luther moderated his views. By the late 1530s, he grudgingly accepted that military resistance by the Protestant states against the emperor might be justified in order to preserve the fledgling Protestant church.[7] He did not, however, abandon his basic commitment to the authority of legitimate political rulers.

This all illustrates Luther's basic political conservatism. Although he was more than willing to challenge the authorities on matters of doctrine, he had no intention of overthrowing society. In fact, given the fact that so many of the powerful figures of his day actually supported his religious reforms, he was well-disposed to support their secular power and to allow them a significant role in the establishment of a reformed church. He was not a revolutionary—except in the intellectual sense.

He was, however, a German. His movement was, from the beginning, deeply connected with the German national consciousness.[8] He often wrote in German in order to appeal to the German public. The popularity of his German writings, and especially the influence of his German translation of the Bible, made Luther the single most influential figure in the development of Modern High German as a literary language.[9] His Address to the Christian Nobility explicitly called upon the German princes to resist the encroachments of a "foreign" papacy. Some of Luther's earliest supporters, in fact, saw Luther's resistance to the church as a potential vehicle for defending German liberties. Thus, the jurist Ulrich von Hutten, for instance, understood Luther's fight against the pope not as a simple theological dispute, but as a war for freedom against tyranny.[10]

And adherence to the new Lutheran form of Christianity came to be a kind of symbol of German identity. The common Catholic faith, which had once been a unifying factor throughout Europe, was now fragmented. Thereafter, religion, which had once been an area of common ground, became a force that separated states from one another.

It is also true that Luther's actions had the effect of putting the state in a position of power over religion. The connection between Luther's religious reforms and his German identity is one of several factors that contributed to the subordination of the German church to the power of the state. At the time, with many of the German princes, including his own rulers in Saxony, embracing Protestantism, Luther may have seen the princes' partial authority over church affairs as an ideal solution. The princes possessed the power necessary to resist Rome, and they could be counted upon to preserve social order. In the long run, however, the substantial role played by the state in church affairs in Germany caused problems. Many historians have suggested that this subordination of the church to the state contributed to the development of authoritarian regimes in Germany during the nineteenth and twentieth centuries.[11]

The most prominent advocate of this position was William Shirer, whose *Rise and Fall of the Third Reich* is one of the most popular histories of Nazi Germany. Shirer writes:

> Through his sermons and his magnificent translation of the Bible, Luther created the modern German language, aroused in the people not only a new Protestant vision of Christianity but a fervent nationalism and taught them, at least in religion, the supremacy of the individual conscience. But, tragically for them, Luther's siding with the princes in the peasant uprisings, which he had largely inspired, and his passion for political autocracy ensure a mindless and provincial absolutism which reduced the vast majority of the German people to poverty, to a horrible torpor and a demeaning subservience.[12]

While Shirer's understanding of Luther's influence on the Nazi era seems to be based on a rather selective reading of Luther, it is true that the German state church—the direct descendant of the Protestant church that Luther helped to found—was unforgivably passive during the Third Reich. But there is more to the story than Shirer recognizes. Although Luther's teachings may have indirectly encouraged a strong German state, Luther can hardly be held responsible for twentieth-century totalitarianism.[13] In fact, Luther's teachings contributed just as significantly to movements of resistance against absolutism. Some of the most prominent resistors to Nazism also drew their ideas from the Lutheran tradition. Dietrich Bonhoeffer, for example, one of the most important Christian opponents of the Nazi regime, was deeply influenced by Luther.[14]

So despite his conservatism and his legacy of support for the state, Luther's ideas can also be seen as contributing to the rise of modern limited governments. John M. Buchanan writes:

> The Reformation led to a full embrace of the radical political implications of a humanity created in the image of God—each individual with God-given dignity and value. And as a consequence it led to political rights, to a new recognition of justice in the civic and political arena, and to a stress on grace as the fundamental word that God has spoken and on gratitude as the essential response of one who has received grace.[15]

Indeed, although he certainly did not understand conscience in quite the same way as modern scholars, Luther's appeal to his own conscience at Worms propagated the idea that the individual conscience could stand up to powerful authorities.[16] Throughout his career, Luther consistently upheld the idea that individuals ought to follow God, even if that forced them to disobey their secular rulers. When asked whether soldiers owed unquestioning allegiance to their commanders, Luther's reply clearly indicated that he believed that it could be appropriate for individuals to resist political authority:

> A second question: "Suppose my lord were wrong in going to war." I reply: If you know for sure that he is wrong, then you should fear God rather than men, and you should neither fight nor serve, for you cannot have a good conscience before God. "Oh, no," you say, "my lord would force me to do it; he would take away my fief and would not give me my money, pay, and wages. Besides, I would be despised and put to shame as a coward, even worse, as a man who did not keep his word and deserted his lord in need." I answer: You must take that risk and, with God's help, let whatever happens, happen.[17]

These ideas lived in some tension with Luther's basic support for the state. But this tension would not have bothered Luther all that much. He was perfectly happy to acknowledge the complexity of human affairs and willing to accept some paradox.

Luther's ideas also contributed to the rise of the modern state in a rather different way. The concept of justification by faith taught that individuals do not need to do anything to merit God's grace. So, in a Lutheran community, there was no longer as strong a need to invest community resources into religious affairs or institutions. And since the state was empowered to participate in religious affairs, certain functions that had previously been fulfilled by the church began to shift toward the state. This refocused some of society's energy in Protestant states. Those resources that had been spent on the afterlife in pre-Reformation Germany could now be freed up for productive use in this life. A great example of this is the development in Germany of government-sponsored schools and social welfare systems. These were functions that the church had historically fulfilled, and that were often available to a limited number of people. Luther suggested that these functions should fall to the state and that their benefits should be distributed more widely. By doing so, Luther encouraged the state to accrue more functions and more power than it had previously enjoyed. This marks the beginning of an important shift in the West toward a centralized state.

7.1.4 Social welfare and education

With regard to social welfare, Luther was pointedly concerned about the plight of the poor and sick. He advocated the creation of a "common chest" – a sort of public fund to support poor relief. He argued that the Bible clearly taught that the community had a responsibility to care for those who could not care for themselves. He did not provide specific instructions about how to distribute the money in the common chest, however. This was left to the judgment of local officials.[18] In addition to empowering the state to act on behalf of the poor, this development clearly foreshadows the modern welfare state.

Luther's advocacy of education also serves to foreshadow modern institutions. The concept of the priesthood of all believers helped to break down the medieval concentration of literacy in the hands of the clergy. If, as Luther asserted, every person has direct access to God, then it became the responsibility of all people to achieve at least enough education to read the Bible for themselves. In 1524, Luther wrote *To the Councilmen of All Cities in Germany that They Establish and Maintain Christian Schools*, a tract that strongly encouraged governments throughout Germany to support public education.[19] An important function of public schools was to equip individuals with the skills necessary for Bible study, so Luther stressed education in the liberal arts and especially in the Biblical languages. In addition to the religious benefits, though, Luther explained to the German princes the importance to society of a well-educated populace:

> It therefore behooves the council and authorities to devote the greatest care and attention to the young. Since the property, honor, and life of the whole city have been committed to their faithful keeping, they would be remiss in their duty before God and man if they did not seek its welfare and improvement day and night with all the means at their command. Now the welfare of a city does not consist solely in accumulating vast treasures, building mighty walls and magnificent buildings, and producing a goodly supply of guns and armor. Indeed, where such things are plentiful and reckless fools get control of them it is so much the worse and the city suffers an even greater loss. A city's best and greatest welfare, safety, and strength consist rather in it having many able, learned, wise, honorable, and well-educated citizens. They can then reliably gather, protect, and properly use treasure and all manner of property.[20]

Luther's associate Melanchthon, who was known to his contemporaries as the "teacher of Germany," went even a step further than this and associated liberal education with the very survival of civilization. Melanchthon insisted that Protestants provide their youth with a thorough education in the classics as a necessary foundation for a good society.[21]

This advocacy of education had a significant effect. Cities and municipalities throughout Germany began to establish schools. Perhaps the most significant piece of evidence demonstrating the impact of Luther on education is the rising literacy rates throughout Protestant Europe in the aftermath of the Reformation.[22]

It is also significant to note that Luther's support for education extended far beyond just basic literacy or even theological training. His ideas also underlay the development of a new model for professional education. Luther was instrumental in developing a professional medical school at Wittenberg. Indeed, his son Paul became a respected doctor.[23] All of this suggests that Luther's conviction that individuals ought to be able to read the Bible and make judgments for themselves led to the development of the modern educational system.

7.1.5 Women and the family

The effects of Luther's thought can also be seen in the changing attitudes toward women and toward the family. Nowhere is this more clearly seen than in his support for clerical marriage. The historian Steven Ozment writes that:

> No institutional change brought about by the Reformation was more visible, responsive to late medieval pleas for reform, and conductive to new social attitudes than in the marriage of Protestant clergy. Nor was there another point in the Protestant program where theology and practice corresponded more successfully [...] In doing so, they extolled as had few before them the virtues of marriage and family life.[24]

Luther's support for clerical marriage led to a number of new developments in European society. It turned the focus in Protestant Europe toward the nuclear family, helped to develop a new respect for domestic labor, and changed the way women participated in both the church and in society at large.

After he married, Luther became an enthusiastic supporter of the family as the basic building block of society. His thought tended to focus on the nuclear family. Thus an effect of the Reformation was to emphasize the nuclear family over the extended, multi-generational clan. The model for the new ideal family was the married pastor and his family, who served to demonstrate the virtues of domestic life to their congregations.[25] Marriage was, for Luther, more than procreation. It involved the creation and nurturing of a family. "Marriage," he said, "does not consist in sleeping with a woman—anybody can do that—but of keeping house and bringing up children."²⁶ This attitude encouraged Luther's followers to see domestic duties like changing diapers and sweeping floors as sacred callings no less pleasing to God than the prayers of monks or the preaching of the gospel from the pulpit. In the 1522 treatise *The Estate of Marriage*, he eloquently described the religious value of domestic life:

> Now observe that when that clever harlot, our natural reason [...] takes a look at married life, she turns up her nose and says, "Alas, must I rock the baby, wash its diapers, make its bed, smell its stench, stay up nights with it, take care of it when it cries, heal its rashes and sores, and on top of that care for my wife, provide for her, labor at my trade, take care of this and take care of that, do this and do that, endure this and endure that, and whatever else of bitterness and drudgery married life involves? What, should I make such a prisoner of myself ...?"
>
> What then does Christian faith say to this? It opens its eyes, looks upon all these insignificant, distasteful, and despised duties in the Spirit, and is aware that they are all adorned with divine approval as with the costliest gold and jewels. It says, "O God, because I am certain that thou hast created me as a man and hast from my body begotten this child, I also know for a certainty that it meets with thy perfect pleasure. I confess to thee that I am not worthy to rock the little babe or wash its diapers, or to be entrusted with the care of the child and its mother [...] O how gladly will I do so, though the duties should be even more insignificant and despised. Neither frost nor heat, neither drudgery nor labor, will distress or dissuade me, for I am certain that it is thus pleasing in thy sight."²⁷

This celebration of domestic duties also forced Luther to recognize the vital role of women in the family and, by extension, in society. Without women, "the home, cities, economic life, and government would disappear. Men can't do without women. Even if it were possible to beget children, they still couldn't do without women."²⁸ This is certainly not an embracing of the modern idea of equality for women, but it does indicate that Luther was coming to see women as something more than second-class citizens.

To be sure, Luther could also be crude and was often misogynistic. He accepted the conventional wisdom of his time that women were weaker than men and were properly suited for keeping house. Thus he could say:

> Men have broad shoulders and narrow hips, and accordingly they possess intelligence. Women have narrow shoulders and broad hips. Women

ought to stay at home; the way they were created indicates this for they have broad hips and a wide fundament to sit upon [to keep house and bear children].[29]

But he was also in many ways ahead of his time when it came to women. For instance, Luther lamented society's tolerance of brothels, and the Protestant communities that followed Luther worked hard to eradicate prostitution.[30] Women were not mere objects of lust, but souls who deserved protection. Furthermore, and perhaps most interesting, Luther broke with tradition by naming Katie in his will as his chief heir and beneficiary. Women were, like minors, not seen as fully legally competent to inherit. But Luther apparently envisioned that Katie would be able to continue as the independent head of the family after his death. This was certainly a radical notion in sixteenth-century Germany.[31] Unfortunately this portion of the will was ruled invalid after Luther's death, and Katie was not allowed to inherit. The incident does show, however, that Luther was willing, under some circumstances, to redefine traditional gender roles.

So it is worthwhile to ask whether Luther's influence was basically positive for women. The question is not easily answered, and one's answer depends substantially on what one chooses to emphasize. On the positive side, Luther's advocacy of clerical marriage opened up a new space for women as pastors' wives, giving them a prominent role in the local congregations. His praise for the religious value of domestic duties allowed women—who were more often than men engaged in those duties—to see their contributions to society as valuable acts of service to God. And the growth in education arising from the Reformation benefited women as well as men.

On the other hand, the Reformation brought about the elimination of monastic orders, which in the middle ages could be a way for women to dedicate themselves to the service of the church while remaining unmarried. The new Protestant world had nothing similar, and marriage was the only option for women. Luther also certainly did not envision a role for women in offices of leadership in the church or in society, and continued to see women's roles in society as primarily traditional.

7.2 Questions about Luther's Legacy

Clearly, Luther's ideas have had a substantial impact on Western civilization. Luther's life and career also raise some important questions. Three of the most significant of those questions are explored below.

7.2.1 Antinomianism—does human behavior matter at all?

One important question raised by Luther's teaching has to do with whether human behavior matters at all. If, as Luther taught, human beings are reconciled to God entirely through God's grace rather than through anything they have done, that might seem to imply that human actions are completely irrelevant. Or, to put it another way, if personal righteousness cannot bring us any closer to God, and if human sins and crimes cannot prevent God from dispensing grace, what reason is there for human beings to live moral lives? It is an important question, and one which Luther's work brings to the fore.

Luther's theology does indeed seem to tend towards a kind of antinomianism—the idea that righteous behavior is unnecessary because the grace of God will save you regardless of your sinfulness. And Luther's bombastic rhetoric sometimes helped to encourage this idea. In a famous letter to Melanchthon, written when he was in hiding at the Wartburg in 1521, he says:

> If you are a preacher of grace, then preach a true and not a fictitious grace; if grace is true, you must bear a true and not a fictitious sin. God does not save people who are only fictitious sinners. Be a sinner and sin boldly, but believe and rejoice in Christ even more boldly, for he is victorious over sin, death, and the world. As long as we are here [in this world] we have to sin. This life is not the dwelling place of righteousness, but, as Peter says, we look for new heavens and a new earth in which righteousness dwells. It is enough that by the riches of God's glory we have come to know the Lamb that takes away the sin of the world. No sin will separate us from the Lamb, even though we commit fornication and murder a thousand times a day. Do you think that the purchase price that was paid for the redemption of our sins by so great a Lamb is too small? Pray boldly—you too are a mighty sinner.[32]

The words "sin boldly" echo from the page. Is Luther suggesting that people should continue to sin, since God will forgive them? If so, then what will happen to the social order? Will human society be able to continue if we all "sin boldly"?

Despite his rhetoric, though, it seems fairly clear that Luther did not, in fact, teach that we should continue to lead dissolute lives. In the first place, his support for the state indicates that he at least believes that people should follow civil laws. But Luther argued, in tension with his "sin boldly" instructions, that striving to live righteously remained a religious duty for Christians. This is perhaps best illustrated by the story of Johan Agricola.

Agricola had been one of Luther's students and was an enthusiastic convert to Protestantism. He was one of Luther's close associates during the early 1520s, until he left Wittenberg to teach in the newly established Protestant school at Eisleben. At this point, he and Luther parted ways a bit. When Luther sent out the visitation teams to check on the quality of the schools and churches in Germany, Agricola objected. Didn't this kind of heavy-handed oversight in effect force churches and schools to adopt Luther's own views? And isn't this kind of forcible change exactly what Luther had refused to allow when Karlstadt tried to impose his own views on Wittenberg?[33] The criticism was a strong one, and Luther was not amused.

It is perhaps because of this earlier run-in with Agricola that Luther's later engagement with him over antinomianism turned particularly ugly. Agricola returned to Wittenberg in 1536. When he did, he was associated with a teaching that claimed that there was no religious reason for Christians to behave righteously, and that therefore the church should not teach or encourage Christians to uphold moral laws as a part of the Christian life. The enforcement of laws and behavior belonged in the secular courts, which were in place to maintain public order. But Christians were, by the grace of God, free from any religious obligation to behave righteously.

Luther's response was vigorous. For him, the moral law was vital to the gospel. Luther's position was that by preaching moral law and by encouraging the congregation to comply with it, the church emphasized that there were moral norms in the universe. Even though human beings could never fully live up to those laws, they should be encouraged to follow them to the best of their abilities. This had two key effects. First, for Luther, preaching the moral law leads people to have faith in Christ. Being presented with the law demonstrates to human beings their inability to follow the law perfectly. And without this knowledge that we cannot—in and of ourselves—live up to God's standards, we cannot come to the faith we need to accept the grace of Christ. Secondly, preaching the moral law gave Christians some guidelines with which to order their lives. While Luther adamantly argued that obeying the law cannot actually save us, he just as vigorously defended the idea that the church needed to preach the law so that Christians would have a guide to good behavior that they could model their lives on. Although keeping these rules could not save you, the absence of law from the Christian life would be disastrous. Luther seems to have seen Agricola as another figure like Karlstadt or Zwingli—he had fundamentally misunderstood the spirit of the gospel by taking it too far.

To understand Luther's interaction with Agricola—and many of his other controversies—it is again helpful to remember that Luther was not particularly concerned with building a completely logical system in which everything fit together neatly. He was comfortable with a little bit of paradox. So it would not have bothered Luther that his key doctrine of justification by faith alone led logically to a kind of antinomianism that he vigorously repudiated.

7.2.2 Why was Luther successful?

Another important question raised by Luther's life and career is why he and the Protestants who followed him were as successful as they were. There had been similar reform movements in the past, none of which had been particularly effective or long-lasting. The most recent popular reformer, Jan Hus, whose teachings had been remarkably similar to Luther's, had been burned at the stake as a heretic at the Council of Constance in 1415. So how did Luther escape this fate? And how did his particular reform movement develop into a worldwide church in a way that Hus' did not? There are several factors to consider.

First, Luther had substantial political support. He was protected by Frederick the Wise, who, in turn, was in a position of uncommon influence in the early sixteenth century. He was also actively supported by a number of German princes who were willing to defy the emperor and the papacy on his behalf. To be sure, their motivations may have had more to do with their political desire to be out from under the authority of the Habsburgs and the papacy, but the fact that they were willing to stand with Luther meant that the church authorities could not simply have Luther arrested and executed—as they had with Hus.

In a similar way, it was deeply important that Luther was popular with the common people. Luther's Catholic opponents regularly found themselves facing angry crowds of Luther's supporters when they tried to enforce disciplinary acts against him. He seems to have had a particular way of engaging the public imagination that encouraged the common people to see him as one of their own. This made the emperor and the pope think twice about arbitrarily arresting Luther for fear of the public outcry.

He was also, in many ways, in the right place at the right time. The forces that opposed Luther were divided and distracted by other affairs. The emperor and the pope were often in conflict with one another and found it challenging to work together against Luther. The growing threat to southern Europe from the Ottoman Turks and wars with France further distracted the emperor. By the time he got around to putting together any significant response to Luther, Luther's ideas were already too well established to be uprooted easily.

Luther also had access to the printing press. This was the state-of-the-art communication technology of the sixteenth century. With printing, Luther's writings could be quickly reproduced and distributed throughout Europe.

This was something completely unavailable to Hus. The authorities could not prevent Luther's writings from getting out. And once those writings were distributed, they attracted followers. Luther also wrote in German, the language of the common people, which further expanded his reach. Even his face was widely recognized because of the portraits of the author that were often printed in the published versions of his works. Thus, Luther became one of the earliest continent-wide celebrities.

Finally, we cannot discount Luther himself. He was, by all accounts, a uniquely charismatic figure. His writings and sermons struck a chord with his listeners in a way that few writers have been able to replicate. He was firm in his dedication to his teachings and was willing to sacrifice everything else for the sake of the gospel. While it may be true that the situation in the sixteenth century was such that a reform of the church was inevitable, there can be little doubt that such a reform would have looked dramatically different if Luther had not been a part of it.

7.2.3 How "Lutheran" was Luther?

Another question raised by the study of Luther is the relationship between Luther himself and the reform movements that drew inspiration from him. In some important ways, Luther differed from other Protestants, and even from those Lutherans who particularly claimed to be his followers.

One of the key things about Luther is the fact that, unlike most of the Protestant reformers, he remained staunchly sacramental. He held to the idea of the sacraments, insisted that Christ was truly, physically present in and through them, and believed that they had real effects on the participant. Although he criticized the Catholic view of the sacraments in *The Babylonian Captivity*, his dispute was not with the concept of the sacraments, but rather with the way in which they were used by the pope. Luther, it seems, came to understand the sacraments in a new way during his conflict with the church, but, far from rejecting them, he became even more focused on the sacraments.[34]

Why was this? It has to do with Luther's distinctive understanding of justification. If, as he argued, justification is an entirely external matter—something Christ does for people rather than something that people earn for themselves—there needed to be some external medium to signify and communicate God's grace. Those external mediums were the sacraments. They were like the wedding ring in a marriage. Even though the ring by itself doesn't serve to make two people married, it serves as an important external symbol of the marriage and gives the wearer a tangible confirmation of his or her status. In the same way, the sacraments, although they did not in and of themselves serve to justify sinners, did give sinners a tangible, real, external symbol of their justification before God. Without such an external symbol, Luther feared, people would begin to see faith as a willful act that a sinner must accomplish in order to be justified. By holding firmly to the real presence and efficacy of the sacraments, Luther emphasized that faith itself was a gift from God.

Philip Cary, one of the most insightful recent commentators on Luther, suggests that this emphasis on the external sacraments makes Luther "not quite Protestant."[35] For Cary, most other Protestants tend to understand faith in such a way that the believer must know that he or she has faith. So faith, for them, comes perilously close to something that the believer must do. At the very least, faith is something that the believer must be aware of having. In some Protestant contexts, the concern over whether one truly has faith can be a cause for a good deal of anxiety. For Luther, on the other hand, the sacraments emphasize that faith is a promise from God. God speaks through the sacrament and promises to grant grace. Such a doctrine—that the sacraments were vital to assure sinners of God's grace—marks Luther as having a rather different theological outlook than many of his fellow Protestants.

In fact, Luther's growing emphasis on the sacraments seems to indicate that Luther was not the theological revolutionary that his Catholic opponents accused him of being. Rather than rejecting the great traditions of the church, Luther was actually returning to a more "Catholic" understanding of the sacraments than the one held by his Catholic opponents.[36] This sacramentalism became even more distinctive for Luther after he broke with the Swiss reformers in 1525, when the belief in the real presence in the sacraments became a distinctive mark of Lutheran identity.

Luther may also be "not quite Protestant" in another way. One of the more interesting recent lines of inquiry about Luther comes out of Finland. In the early 1970s a group of Luther researchers at the University of Helsinki, led by Tuomo Mannermaa, began working closely with the Russian Orthodox community in Finland. As a part of their attempts to find common theological ground with the Orthodox, Mannermaa and his colleagues began to suggest that Luther's writings support the Orthodox teaching of *theosis*—the idea that the Christian believer actually becomes, through faith, united with God.[37]

This was, and remains, a controversial conclusion. Traditionally, Lutherans have taught that God's grace *declares* the sinner to be righteous, but does not actually *make* the sinner righteous—an idea that Lutherans know as "forensic justification." Thus Christians can be at the same time righteous and sinful. The Finnish scholars would set aside this understanding of declared righteousness and instead suggest that Luther's understanding of justification, like the Orthodox doctrine of *theosis*, involves the sinner being actually changed and made righteous. Many Lutheran theologians reject the Finnish school, suggesting that Mannermaa's desire to find common ground with the Orthodox may have led him to read ideas into Luther's writings that Luther himself would find alien.[38] Others support the Finnish school, pointing out that a man like Luther, who conscientiously held to the real presence in the sacraments, may very well have been sympathetic to the idea that the grace of God could produce real results in the sinful soul.

A final word is in order about Luther's relationship with Lutheranism. After Luther died in 1546, leadership of the Lutheran community in Wittenberg passed to Philip Melanchthon. Soon, a group that became known as the "Gnesio-Lutherans" ("true Lutherans") began to accuse Melanchthon of betraying Luther's ideals. It was the first of many conflicts between Luther's successors over the precise meaning and content of Luther's heritage. Melanchthon, who was by nature an irenic person, had little of Luther's taste for controversy. As such, he was more willing to talk with—and, at least in the eyes of his opponents, to compromise with—non-Lutheran Protestants than Luther had been. The Gnesio-Lutherans accused Melanchthon of downplaying the importance of the real presence in the sacraments and of compromising on the doctrine of justification by faith alone by suggesting that human beings could cooperate in their own salvation.[39] Melanchthon's followers, who came to be known as the "Philippists," defended him, claiming that Luther himself would certainly endorse all of Melanchthon's teachings. The schism that developed saw both sides claiming that their own views were truly those of Luther, while those of their opponents were a dangerous betrayal of the great man's legacy.

Whether the Philippists or the Gnesio-Lutherans were right about Luther isn't really significant for our purposes. What is clear from the controversy is that Luther's own friends and students—men and women who had known Luther personally—could disagree about the details of Luther's thinking. This, in and of itself, should serve to illustrate that the followers of Luther may or may not fully reflect the views of Luther himself. So, in this sense as well, Luther may be "not quite Protestant."

7.3 Concluding Thoughts

I began this study with Luther's declaration that:

> I am the son of a peasant. My great-grandfather, grandfather, and father were peasants [...] I should have become a superintendent, a bailiff or the like in the village, a servant with authority over a few [...] that I [earned a good education], that I became a monk which brought shame

upon me as it bitterly annoyed my father—that I and the Pope came to blows, that I married an apostate nun; who would have read this in the stars? Who would have prophesied it?[40]

He was absolutely right in this assessment. Nobody could have predicted how the peasant's son from Saxony would become one of the most significant figures in European history. We too should be surprised at how dramatic Luther's influence was. In addition to the obvious effects of religious division and changing theological ideas, Luther's life and writings influenced the development of the German language, served to promote new ideas about government and about the value of the individual, and changed people's ideas about marriage and the family. His impact is felt in the realms of art and music, and his name and face are recognizable to millions of people nearly five hundred years later. He was truly a revolutionary figure.

But, in a very important way, he was an accidental revolutionary. He was a man who discovered an important and life-changing idea—the gospel of justification by faith. His entire career was built upon the stubborn desire to spread this gospel in the face of any opposition. He had no desire to split the church, to oppose the emperor, to become a German national hero, or to change the way people lived. This was all completely unintended. But, in the course of boldly proclaiming the gospel that he had discovered, he accomplished all of these things and more.

FOR FURTHER STUDY

There is an enormous number of books about Luther, and tens of thousands of articles appearing in both popular and scholarly journals. The following is intended to guide those who might want to explore Luther and his world more deeply.

Every serious student of Luther should read Luther's own works. Most are easily available in English translation. The standard scholarly edition in English is the 55-volume *Luther's Works*, known commonly as the "American Edition" (Concordia/Fortress, 1955–1986). This is the most complete collection of Luther's writings available in English, and is commonly held by larger libraries. It is also available in a CD-ROM edition, which has the distinct advantage of being searchable by computer. John Dillenberger, *Martin Luther: Selections from his Writings* (Anchor Books, 1961) and Timothy Lull, *Martin Luther's Basic Theological Writings* (Augsburg, 2005) are both good one-volume compilations. Many of Luther's key works are also available online through the Project Wittenberg website (www.projectwittenberg.org).

There are literally thousands of biographies of Luther, and not all are worth reading. Martin Brecht's three-volume *Martin Luther* (Fortress Press, 1985–1993) is widely considered to be the scholarly standard. James Kittelson, *Martin Luther the Reformer* (Augsburg, 1986) and Derek Wilson, *Out of the Storm* (St. Martin's, 2007) are both readable single-volume treatments. Once considered a standard, Roland Bainton, *Here I Stand* (Abingdon, 1950) now seems a bit dated, but can still be valuable. Bernhard Lohse, *Martin Luther: An Introduction to His Life and Work* (Fortress, 1986) is not a biography in the traditional sense, but rather an outline and summary of the key topics and issues in Luther's career. Heiko Oberman, *Luther: The Man Between God and the Devil* (Yale, 1989) is powerful, but can be difficult. Many shorter biographies only cover portions of Luther's life. Some of the more helpful of these are

Heinrich Boehmer, *Martin Luther: His Road to Reformation* (Meridian, 1957), Heinrich Bornkamm, *Luther in Mid-Careeer, 1521–1530* (Fortress, 1983) and H. G. Haile, *Luther: An Experiment in Biography* (Princeton, 1983).

To get a sense of the broader picture of the reformation and Luther's place in the larger movement, Carter Lindberg, *The European Reformations* (Blackwell, 1986) and Euan Cameron, *The European Reformation* (Clarendon, 1991) are very helpful. Steven Ozment, *The Age of Reform* (Yale, 1981) is a brilliant guide to the theological atmosphere in which Luther lived and worked. Patrick Collinson, *The Reformation: A History* (Modern Library, 2003) is a short, but remarkably complete, survey of the entire reformation movement.

For Luther's theology, I found Oswald Bayer, *Martin Luther's Theology: A Contemporary Interpretation* (Eerdmans, 2008) to be particularly helpful. Bernhard Lohse, *Martin Luther's Theology: Its Historical and Systematic Development* (Fortress, 1999) and Paul Althaus, *The Theology of Martin Luther* (Fortress, 1966) are both thorough surveys of Luther's thought. Robert Kolb and Charles P. Arand, *The Genius of Luther's Theology* (Baker Academic, 2008) is a readable and interesting book.

Two recent books about the long-term impact of Luther's ideas are well worth considering. Alister McGrath, *Christianity's Dangerous Idea* (HarperOne, 2008) and Brad Gregory, *The Unintended Reformation* (Harvard, 2012) both connect the ideas of the reformation to contemporary issues.

The 2003 film *Luther*, directed by Eric Till, is a generally accurate, sympathetic portrayal of Luther's early career and conflict with the papacy. If you can, you should also watch the Louis de Rochemont film *Martin Luther* from 1953.

The Teaching Company has released a series of audio lectures on Luther's life and thought by Philip Cary, and they are an excellent introduction to the subject.

NOTES

Introduction

1 Lohse, *Martin Luther*, 20.

Chapter 1. Context

1 Friedman, "The Life Millennium," 162.
2 Hillerbrand, *The Reformation*, 22.
3 Matthew 16:19.

Chapter 2. Luther's Early Life

1 LW 54:235; see also 54:157; 54:457.
2 Erikson, *Young Man Luther*.
3 See, for instance, Ozment, *The Age of Reform*, 223–231; Lindbeck, "Erikson's Young Man Luther"; Spitz, "Psychohistory and History."
4 See, for instance, LW 48:329–336 and 49:267–271.
5 Cited in Oberman, *Luther*, 120.
6 Ozment, *The Age of Reform*, 233–235; McGrath, *Intellectual Origins of the European Reformation*, 79–80.
7 LW 31:129–130.
8 Hillerbrand, *The Reformation*, 23.
9 LW 54:109.
10 LW 54:338.
11 LW 54:339–340.
12 LW 27:13.
13 LW 34:336.
14 LW 54:232.
15 LW 8:182.
16 LW 54:237.
17 LW 34:336.
18 LW 10:407.

19 See Lohse, *Martin Luther*, 149–153 for a summary of the arguments for both the early- and late-dating positions.
20 LW 34:336–337.

Chapter 3. The Accidental Reformer

1 LW 31:18–35.
2 Hillerbrand, *The Reformation*, 42–43.
3 For instance, in LW 10:351, 25:409, and 51:26–41.
4 The key text is Iserloh, *The Theses Were Not Posted*.
5 LW 31:25–33.
6 Brecht, *Martin Luther: His Road to Reformation*, 204–205.
7 Cited in Lindberg, *The European Reformations*, 78.
8 LW 54:83.
9 LW 31:63.
10 LW 31:40.
11 See Forde, *On Being a Theologian of the Cross*.
12 LC 1:80; see also Greschat, *Martin Bucer*, 27–31.
13 LC 1:85.
14 Cited in Kittelson, *Luther the Reformer*, 121.
15 LW 31:274–275.
16 LC 1:120.
17 Cited in Estep, *Renaissance and Reformation*, 127.
18 LC 1:293–294.
19 LC 1:349.
20 LW 44:115–217.
21 LW 44:137.
22 LC 1:344.
23 LW 44:123–217.
24 See Bayer, *Martin Luther's Theology*, 50ff.
25 Boehmer, *Martin Luther*, 328.
26 Boehmer, *Martin Luther*, 324.
27 LW 31:333–377.
28 LW 31:333.
29 LW 31:345.
30 LW 31:373.
31 LC 1:423.
32 LC 1:455.
33 Cited in Kittelson, *Luther the Reformer*, 159.
34 LW 48: 199–200.
35 LW 32:101.
36 LW 32:101.

Chapter 4. Conflict and Reform

1 Hillerbrand, *The Reformation*, 381.
2 LW 54:280.

3 LW 48:257.
4 LW 35:188.
5 Lohse, *Martin Luther*, 118.
6 See Brecht, *Martin Luther: Shaping and Defining the Reformation*, 46–56.
7 LW 48:365–66
8 LW 51:72.
9 LW 51:91.
10 Cited in Kittelson, *Luther the Reformer*, 183.
11 Ozment, *Age of Reform*, 272–280; Hillerbrand, *The Reformation*, 389–391.
12 LW 46:19.
13 LW 46:30.
14 LW 46:50.
15 Scott and Scribner, *The German Peasants War*, 322–324.
16 LW 46:73ff.
17 Von Loewenich, *Martin Luther*, 266.
18 LW 48:116.
19 LW 48:24, 48:40, 48:53.
20 Von Loewenich, *Martin Luther*, 266.
21 Rupp, *Luther and Erasmus*, 35–99.
22 Rupp, *Luther and Erasmus*, 35.
23 Rupp, *Luther and Erasmus*, 41.
24 Rupp, *Luther and Erasmus*, 91.
25 Cited in Von Loewenich, *Martin Luther: The Man and His Work*, 267.
26 LW 33.
27 LW 50:171–172.
28 LW 33:289.
29 LW 33:65.
30 Bainton, *Erasmus of Christendom*, 190.
31 LW 33:293.
32 See Moeller, *Imperial Cities and the Reformation*, 42ff.
33 Dixon, "The Princely Reformation in Germany," 155–156.
34 LW 49:297.
35 Reu, *The Augsburg Confession*.
36 See, for instance, Dulles, "The Catholicity of the Augsburg Confession."
37 Lindberg, *The European Reformations*, 239–240.

Chapter 5. A New Way to Be a Christian

1 LW 34:336–337.
2 Cited in Hendrix, "Luther," 40.
3 LW 31:104.
4 See, for instance, LW 27:230.
5 See Althaus, *The Theology of Martin Luther*, 242–245.
6 See McGrath, *Christianity's Dangerous Idea*, 208–213.
7 Ozment, *The Reformation in the Cities*, 116.
8 LW 44:123.
9 Wilson, "The Luther Legacy," 35.
10 LW 36:11ff.

11 See Yeago, "The Catholic Luther," 25–33.
12 Astute readers will recognize the similarity between Luther's position here and that laid out by St. Augustine in *The City of God*.
13 Thompson, "Luther and the Right of Resistance."
14 LW 44:175–179.
15 LW 44:174.
16 LW 36:75–77.
17 LW 49:93.
18 Treu, "Katharina von Bora;" see also Brecht, *Martin Luther: Shaping and Defining the Reformation*, 195ff.
19 Brecht, *Martin Luther: Shaping and Defining the Reformation*, 196.
20 Hillerbrand, *The Reformation*, 393–394.
21 LC 2:325.
22 LW 49:117.
23 LW 49:117.
24 LC 2:325.
25 LW 54:7
26 Treu, "Katharina von Bora," 162.
27 LW 53:15.
28 BC 345–377.
29 LW 50:172.
30 LW 53:15–40.
31 LW 53:51–90.
32 LW 53:321.
33 LW 53:37.

Chapter 6. The Final Years

1 Hillerbrand, *The Reformation*, 398.
2 LW 54:432.
3 Von Loewenich, *Martin Luther*, 286.
4 Cited in Edwards, *Luther's Last Battles*, 6.
5 See, e.g. Haile, *Luther*, 221.
6 See Edwards, *Luther's Last Battles*, 6–19.
7 See Brecht, *Martin Luther: The Preservation of the Church*, 333–334.
8 LW 22:366.
9 Edwards, *Luther's Last Battles*, 97–114.
10 LW 43:213–241.
11 Brecht, *Martin Luther: The Preservation of the Church*, 354.
12 LW 46:183ff.
13 LW 45:199–229.
14 LW 45:200.
15 Cited in Brecht, *Martin Luther: The Preservation of the Church*, 337.
16 LW 54:239.
17 LW 47:176.
18 LW 47:268–272.
19 See Gritsch, *Martin Luther's Anti-Semitism*.
20 See Siemon-Netto, *The Fabricated Luther*.

21 Smith, "Luther and Henry VIII," 665–666.
22 LW 50:242.
23 LW 50:290.
24 LW 50:300.
25 LW 50:302.
26 LW 51:381.
27 LW 54:476.
28 Kusukawa, *Orations on Philosophy and Education*, 261.
29 Kusukawa, *Orations on Philosophy and Education*, 253.
30 Cited in Greschat, *Martin Bucer*, 207–208.

Chapter 7. The World Luther Made

1 Dickens, *The English Reformation*, 339.
2 See Larson, *Reforming the North*.
3 Wilson, *Out of the Storm*, 344.
4 Marty, "Luther's Living Legacy," 53.
5 Ozment, "Luther's Political Legacy," 22ff.
6 See, i.e. LW 27:418, 45:91.
7 See Cargill-Thompson, "Luther and the Right of Resistance," and Schoenberger, "Luther and the Justifiability of Resistance."
8 See Oberman, *Luther*, 40–41.
9 Sanders, *German: A Biography*, 117–151. See also Haile, *Luther*, 329–340.
10 LC I:349, I:354–5.
11 See McGrath, *Reformation Thought*, 214 and Ozment, *Protestants*, 119ff.
12 Shirer, *Rise and Fall of the Third Reich*, 91.
13 See Siemon-Netto, *Fabricated Luther* for a detailed response to Shirer's position.
14 Rumscheidt, "Formation of Bonhoeffer's Theology," 50–70.
15 Buchanan, "Luther's Legacy," 3.
16 LW 32:112–113.
17 LW 46:130.
18 LW 45:169–176.
19 LW 45:339–378.
20 LW 45:355–356.
21 Ozment, *Age of Reform*, 311.
22 Maag, "Education and Literacy," 542–543.
23 Lindberg, *The European Reformations*, 373.
24 Ozment, *Age of Reform*, 381.
25 Karant-Nunn, "Reformation Society, Women and the Family," 433–439.
26 LW 54:441.
27 LW 45:40.
28 LW 54:161.
29 LW 54:8. See also Karant-Nunn and Wiesner-Hanks, *Luther on Women*, 15–31.
30 LW 44:214ff. See also Lindberg, *The European Reformations*, 365–366.
31 Stjerna, *Women and the Reformation*, 66.
32 LW 48:282.
33 Kittelson, *Luther the Reformer*, 214–215.
34 Yeago, "The Catholic Luther," 25.

35 Cary, "Why Luther is Not Quite Protestant," Cary, "Sola Fide."
36 Yeago, "The Catholic Luther," 26.
37 Mannermaa, "Why is Luther so Fascinating?," 1–20. See also Mannermaa, *Christ Present in Faith* and Mannermaa, *Two Kinds of Love*.
38 See, for instance, Kolb, *Martin Luther*, 127–129.
39 Manschreck, *Melanchthon*, 293–301.
40 Hillerbrand, *The Reformation*, 22.

BIBLIOGRAPHY

Abbreviations for commonly cited works:

BC *The Book of Concord: The Confessions of the Evangelical Lutheran Church*, ed. Robert Kolb and Timothy J. Wengert. Minneapolis: Fortress, 2000.
LC *Luther's Correspondence and Other Contemporary Letters*, ed. Preserved Smith, 2 vols. Philadelphia: Lutheran Publication Society, 1914–1918.
LW *Luther's Works*, ed. Jaroslav Pelikan and Helmut T. Lehmann, 55 vols. St. Louis: Concordia / Philadelphia: Fortress, 1955–1986.

Althaus, Paul. *The Theology of Martin Luther*. Philadelphia: Fortress Press, 1966.
Bainton, Roland H. *Erasmus of Christendom*. New York: Scribner, 1969.
Bayer, Oswald. *Martin Luther's Theology: A Contemporary Introduction*. Grand Rapids: Eerdmans, 2008.
Boehmer, Heinrich. *Martin Luther: Road to Reformation*. Philadelphia: Muhlenberg, 1946.
Brecht, Martin. *Martin Luther: His Road to Reformation, 1483–1521*. Minneapolis: Fortress Press, 1985.
———. *Martin Luther: Shaping and Defining the Reformation, 1521–1532*. Minneapolis: Fortress Press, 1994.
———. *Martin Luther: The Preservation of the Church, 1532–1546*. Minneapolis: Fortress Press, 1999.
Buchanan, John M. "Luther's Legacy," *The Christian Century*, Oct. 17 2012, 3.
Cargill Thompson, W. D. J. "Luther and the Right of Resistance to the Emperor." In *Church, Society and Politics: Papers Read at the 13th Summer Meeting and 14th Winter Meeting of the Ecclesiastical History Society*. Ed. Derek Baker. Oxford: Basil Blackwell, 1975.
Cary, Phillip. "Sola Fide: Luther and Calvin." *Concordia Theological Quarterly* 71 (2007): 265–281.
———. "Why Luther Is Not Quite Protestant: The Logic of Faith in a Sacramental Promise." *Pro Ecclesia* 14 (2005): 447–486.
Dickens, A. G. *The English Reformation*. New York: Schocken Books, 1964.
Dixon, C. Scott. "The Princely Reformation in Germany." In Andrew Pettegree, ed., *The Reformation World*. London: Routledge, 2000.
Dulles, Avery. "The Catholicity of the Augsburg Confession." *The Journal of Religion* 63, no. 4 (1983): 337–354.

Edwards, Mark U. *Luther's Last Battles: Politics and Polemics, 1531–1543*. Minneapolis: Fortress Press, 1983.
Erikson, Erik H. *Young Man Luther: A Study in Psychoanalysis and History*. New York: Norton, 1958.
Estep, William R. *Renaissance and Reformation*. Grand Rapids: Eerdmans, 1986.
Friedman, Robert, ed. *The Life Millennium: The 100 Most Important Events and People of the Past 1000 Years*. New York: Bulfinch Press, 1998.
Greschat, Martin. *Martin Bucer: A Reformer and His Times*. Louisville: Westminster John Knox, 2004.
Gritsch, Eric W. *Martin Luther's Anti-Semitism: Against His Better Judgment*. Grand Rapids: Eerdmans, 2012.
Haile, H. G. *Luther: An Experiment in Biography*. Princeton: Princeton University Press, 1980.
Hendrix, Scott. "Luther." In David Bagchi and David C. Steinmetz, eds., *The Cambridge Companion to Reformation Theology*. Cambridge: Cambridge University Press, 2004.
Hillerbrand, Hans, ed. *The Reformation: A Narrative History Related by Contemporary Observers and Participants*. Grand Rapids: Baker Book House, 1972.
Iserloh, Erwin. *The Theses Were Not Posted: Luther Between Reform and Reformation*. Boston: Beacon Press, 1968.
Karant-Nunn, Susan C. "Reformation Society, Women and the Family." In Andrew Pettegree, ed., *The Reformation World*. London: Routledge, 2000.
Karant-Nunn, Susan C. and Wiesner-Hanks, Merry E., eds. *Luther on Women: A Sourcebook*. Cambridge: Cambridge University Press, 2003.
Kittelson, James M. *Luther the Reformer*. Minneapolis: Augsburg, 1984.
Kolb, Robert. *Martin Luther: Confessor of the Faith*. Oxford: Oxford University Press, 2009.
Larson, James L. *Reforming the North: The Kingdoms and Churches of Scandinavia, 1520–1545*. Cambridge: Cambridge University Press, 2010.
Lindbeck, George A. "Erickson's Young Man Luther: A Historical and Theological Appraisal." *Soundings* 56 (1973): 210–227.
Lindberg, Carter. *The European Reformations*. Oxford: Blackwell, 1996.
Lohse, Bernhard. *Martin Luther: An Introduction to His Life and Work*. Philadelphia: Fortress Press, 1986.
Maag, Karin. "Education and Literacy." In Andrew Pettegree, ed., *The Reformation World*. London: Routledge, 2000.
Mannermaa, Tuomo. "Why is Luther So Fascinating? Modern Finnish Luther Research." In Carl E. Braaten and Robert W. Jenson, eds, *Union With Christ: The New Finnish Interpretation of Luther*. Grand Rapids: Eerdmans, 1998.
———. *Christ Present in Faith: Luther's View of Justification*. Minneapolis: Fortress, 2005.
———. *Two Kinds of Love: Martin Luther's Religious World*. Minneapolis: Fortress, 2010.
Manschreck, Clyde L. *Melanchthon: The Quiet Reformer*. Nashville: Abingdon, 1958.
Marty, Martin. "Luther's Living Legacy." *Christian History* 39 (1993): 51–53.
McGrath, Alister. *Christianity's Dangerous Idea: The Protestant Revolution—a History from the Sixteenth Century to the Twenty-First*. New York: HarperOne, 2007.
———. *Reformation Thought: An Introduction*. Oxford: John Wiley and Sons, 2012.
Moeller, Bernd. *Imperial Cities and the Reformation: Three Essays*. Durham, NC: Labyrinth Press, 1982.
Oberman, Heiko A. *Luther: Man Between God and the Devil*. New Haven: Yale University Press, 1989.
Ozment, Steven. *The Age of Reform, 1250–1550: An Intellectual and Religious History of Late Medieval and Reformation Europe*. New Haven: Yale University Press, 1980.

———. "Luther's Political Legacy." In James F. Harris, ed., *German-American Interrelations: Heritage and Challenge*. Tubingen: Tubingen University Press, 1985.

———. *Protestants: The Birth of a Revolution*. New York: Image Books, 1993.

Reu, Johann Michael. *The Augsburg Confession: A Collection of Sources*. St. Louis: Concordia Seminary Press, 1966.

Rumscheidt, Martin. "The Formation of Bonhoeffer's Theology." In John W. de Gruchy, ed., *The Cambridge Companion to Dietrich Bonhoeffer*. Cambridge: Cambridge University Press, 1999.

Rupp, Ernest Gordon, ed. *Luther and Erasmus: Free Will and Salvation*. Louisville: Westminster John Knox, 1969.

Sanders, Ruth H. *German: A Biography of a Language*. Oxford: Oxford University Press, 2010.

Scott, Tom and Scribner, Bob, eds. *The German Peasants' War: A History in Documents*. Atlantic Highlands NJ: Humanities Press International, 1991.

Shirer, William L. *The Rise and Fall of the Third Reich: A History of Nazi Germany*. New York: Simon and Schuster, 1960.

Shoenberger, Cynthia Grant. "Luther and the Justifiability of Resistance to Legitimate Authority." *Journal of the History of Ideas* 40 (1979): 3–20.

Siemon-Netto, Uwe. *The Fabricated Luther: Refuting Nazi Connections and Other Modern Myths*. St Louis: Concordia, 2007.

Smith, Preserved. "Luther and Henry VIII." *English Historical Review* 25 (1910): 656–669.

Spitz, Lewis W. "Psychohistory and History: The Case of Young Man Luther." In Roger A. Johnson, ed., *Psychohistory and Religion: The Case of Young Man Luther*. Philadelphia: Fortress Press, 1977.

Stjerna, Kirsi. *Women and the Reformation*. Oxford: Blackwell, 2009.

Treu, Martin. "Katharina von Bora: The Woman at Luther's Side." *Lutheran Quarterly* 13 (1999): 157–178.

von Loewenich, Walther. *Martin Luther: The Man and His Work*. Minneapolis: Augsburg, 1982.

Wilson, Derek. "The Luther Legacy." *History Today* 57 (2007): 34–39.

———. *Out of the Storm: The Life and Legacy of Martin Luther*. New York: Macmillan, 2008.

Yeago, David. "The Catholic Luther." In Carl E. Braaten and Robert W. Jenson, eds., *The Catholicity of the Reformation*. Grand Rapids: Eerdmans, 1996.

INDEX

African Protestantism 92
Agricola, Johann 102–4
Albert of Mainz 26–28
Albrecht III 88
Aleander, Jerome 37, 43
American Protestantism 92
Amsdorf, Nicholas 74
antinomianism 102–4
Aquinas 68
Augsburg Confession 62–63
Augustine, St. 58, 114
Augustinian order 18–19, 28–30, 33, 74

Bainton, Roland 59
baptism 6–7, 40, 49, 51, 70
Benedict XVI 63
Bernard of Clairvaux 33, 89
Bible 2, 19–20, 29, 34, 36, 55–56, 59–60, 66, 98–99
    authority of scripture 33, 36, 51–52, 67–69, 93
    Galatians 20
    humanist reading 11
    King James Bible 48
    Luke 47
    Luther's German translation 48, 80, 95–96
    Psalms 19–21, 77
    Revelation 40, 46
    Romans 20–21, 71
    vernacular translation 10, 48
    Vulgate 47

Biel, Gabriel 16
bigamy 86–87
bishops 7
Black Death 8–9
Boehmer, Heinrich 41
Bora, Katherina von; *see* Luther, Katherina
Bucer, Martin 31, 55, 87, 90
Buchanan, John M. 96

Cajetan 32–37, 68
Calvin, John 57
Capitio, Wolfgang 84
cardinals 7
Cary, Philip 106
celibacy of clergy 49, 62, 72–75, 81, 99, 101
Charles V (Charles of Spain) 32, 37, 43–44, 46, 50, 56, 60–63, 71, 83, 86–87, 95, 104, 108
Christian II 92
church music 77–78
Clement V 9
Clement VII 10
conciliarism 6–7, 10, 29, 34
confession 7–8, 18, 24, 40, 62
Council of Constance 10, 31, 36, 104

Dickens, A. G. 91
Diet of Augsburg 62–63
Diet of Speyer (1526) 61–62
Diet of Speyer (1529) 62

Diet of Worms 43–45, 61, 68, 71, 96
disputations 23; *see also* Luther, Martin (works): *95 Theses*
Dominican order 29, 33
Durer, Albrecht 46

Eck, Johannes 34–37, 68
education 15, 68, 91, 98–99, 101
Eisenach 15, 46
Eisleben 5, 13, 88, 103
Emser, Hieronymus 48
England 10, 92
Erasmus, Desiderius 11, 28, 54, 57–60, 67, 86, 89
  On the Freedom of the Will 58–59
Erfurt 15–20, 30, 35
Erikson, Erik 14–17
Eucharist 7–8, 18, 40, 49, 51–52, 55–57, 62, 70, 76–77
Evangelicals 65

famine 8
Ferdinand of Austria 61
Fifth Lateran Council 7
forensic justification 106
Frederick the Great 48
Frederick the Wise 25, 32, 34–37, 41–43, 45–46, 50, 60–61, 71, 75, 104
free will 58–60, 67

George of Saxony 35–36, 61
German nationalism 37–38
Gnesio-Lutherans 107
Goethe, Johann Wolfgang von 48
Gregorian chant 49
Gregory VII 9

Habsburg dynasty 32, 34, 37, 104
Heidelberg disputation 30–31, 34, 55, 90
Henry VIII 74, 87
  Defense of the Seven Sacraments 41
Holland 92
Holy Roman Empire 12, 32, 36–37, 39, 48, 87; *see also* Charles V
humanism 11, 26, 37, 57, 59
Hus, Jan 10–11, 31–32, 35–36, 104–5
Hutten, Ulrich von 37–39, 95

iconoclasm 49, 52
individualism 11, 69–70, 91, 93–94, 96–97, 108
indulgences 23–30, 36, 67
  plenary 25
Ingolstadt 34
Islam 83

Jeremiah 89
Jesus Christ 6, 30–31, 35, 40–42, 49, 51, 53, 60, 65–68, 84, 89, 103, 105
John (apostle) 46
John Frederick 84
John the Baptist 89
John the Steadfast 61–63, 75–76
Josel of Rosheim 84
Judaism 84–86
justification by faith alone 21, 40–42, 45, 49, 51, 55, 60, 65–67, 72, 83, 93, 97, 105, 107–8; *see also* antinomianism; forensic justification; *theosis*

Karlstadt, Andreas 33–35, 48–51, 54, 56, 68, 94, 103

Leipzig debate 35–37, 48
Lent 55
Leo X 26–29, 32, 34, 36–38, 41, 43
Link, Wenceslaus 88
Lohse, Bernhard 2
Lotzer, Sebastian 52
Luther, Elizabeth 80
Luther, Hans 5, 13, 18–19
Luther, Katherina 73–75, 80–81, 88, 101
Luther, Magdalena 80
Luther, Margaret 5, 14
Luther, Martin (life)
  anfechtung 16–17
  appeal to Leo X 33–34
  Augsburg examination 32–33
  birth 13
  charge of heresy 29–31, 33–35, 37, 42–43
  childhood 14–15
  death 88–90
  declining health 81–82
  education 15–16
  excommunication 33, 37–38, 42, 57
  family life 79–81

marriage 72–75, 79, 99
monkhood 17–19
musical abilities 77, 81
professorship 19–21, 23
summons to Rome 29, 31–32
Wartburg exile 45–46, 56, 68, 102
Luther, Martin (works); *see also Table Talk*
   95 Theses 23–30, 34, 55, 58, 67, 89
   Address to the Christian Nobility 38–41,
     47, 69, 72, 95
   Admonition to Peace 53–54
   Against the Robbing and Murdering
     Hordes of Peasants 53–54
   Babylonian Captivity of the Church 38,
     40–41, 70, 72, 105
   Bondage of the Will 59–60, 76
   Catechisms 76
   Estate of Marriage 100
   Explanations of the 95 Theses 66
   Mighty Fortress 77
   On the Freedom of a Christian 38, 41–42
   On the Jews and Their Lies 85
   Open Letter on the Harsh Book Against
     the Peasants 54
   That Jesus Christ was Born a Jew 84–85
   To the Councilmen of All Cities in
     Germany that They Establish and
     Maintain Christian Schools 98
Lutheran church organization 75–77

Mannermaa, Tuomo 106
Mansfield 13, 15, 17, 88
Marburg Colloquy 56, 86
marriage (institution) 99–100, 108
marriage (sacrament) 6
Maximilian I 32, 34
Mazzolini, Sylvester; *see* Prierias
Medici 27
Melanchthon, Philip 26, 38, 46, 48,
   62–63, 73, 87, 89, 92, 98, 102, 107
Miltitz, Karl von 41
monks 7, 72; *see also* Augustinian order;
   Dominican order; celibacy of clergy;
   nuns
More, Thomas 28

nationalism 95
Nazis 96

Nietzsche, Friedrich 48
nominalism 16–17, 20
nuns 7, 72–73; *see also* Augustinian order;
   celibacy of clergy; Dominican order;
   monks
Nuremberg 12, 63

original sin 7, 20
Ottoman Empire 83, 104
Ozment, Steven 69, 99

papacy 6–7, 14, 27, 34, 37, 44, 58, 61, 65,
   75, 86, 95, 104; *see also* Leo X
   authority 10–12, 28–29, 31, 33–37, 47,
     52, 66–67
   Avignon papacy 9–10
   celibacy of clergy 80
   conflict with Luther 38, 46, 48, 60,
     82–83, 86, 95, 104, 108
   corruption 10
   indulgences 25–26
   infallibility 29, 68
   sacraments 40, 105
   schism 9–10
Paul (apostle) 50, 89
peasant revolts 9
   Peasants' War 52–54, 61, 68, 71, 94
penance 8, 23–24, 27, 40, 66
Peter (apostle) 6, 102
Petri, Laurentius 92
Petri, Olaus 92
Philip of Hesse 86–87
Philippists 107
Pius II 34
Prierias 29, 32–34, 36
priesthood of all believers 11, 49, 69–70,
   93, 98
priests 7
printing 28, 38, 48, 104–5
prostitution 101
Protestant princes 62, 71, 95
purgatory 24–25

Reformation 3, 5, 36, 39, 65, 77, 91
Renaissance 11, 27, 59
Reutlingen 63
righteousness 20–21, 30, 41–42, 66–67,
   83, 102–4, 106–7

sacraments 7–8, 40–41, 50, 55, 58, 70, 105–7; *see also* baptism; Eucharist; marriage; penance
Scandinavian Protestantism 92
Schappeler, Christoph 52
scholastic theology 28, 30–31, 37, 67, 84
Scotland 92
Shakespeare, William 48, 92
Shirer, William 96
social welfare 97–98
Spalatin, George 31, 39, 72
Staupitz, Johann von 18–19, 28, 43
Swedish Protestantism 92
Switzerland 55, 92

Table Talk 2, 81, 83
Tetzel, John 24–29, 31–32, 67
theosis 106–7
Theses; *see* Luther, Martin (works): 95 Theses
Torgau 62
transubstantiation 40, 50

Twelve Articles 52–53
'two kingdoms' principle 71
Tyndale, William 48

Urban VI 9

Vasa, Gustavus 92

Wartburg; *see under* Luther, Martin
Wesel, Johannes von 16
William of Occam 16
Wilson, Derek 69, 93
Wittenberg 19, 23, 25–26, 29, 32, 34, 37, 42, 44–46, 48, 55, 72–73, 75, 79–81, 89, 92, 99, 103, 107
  reform movement 46, 48–52, 54–55
women's social roles 100–101
Wyclif, John 10, 31

"Zwickau prophets" 49–51, 56, 68, 83
Zwilling, Gabriel 49
Zwingli, Ulrich 54–57, 70, 77, 83, 86, 103

www.ingramcontent.com/pod-product-compliance
Lightning Source LLC
Chambersburg PA
CBHW020126240426
43673CB00038B/608